BUSINESS IN RED SHOES
THE SUCCESSFUL BUSINESS
WOMAN'S GUIDE

BY REBECCA JONES

Paperback ISBN 978-1-907685-96-5
ePub ISBN 978-1-907685-97-2
Mobipocket/Kindle ISBN 978-1-907685-98-9
Published in the UK by MX Publishing
335 Princess Park Manor, Royal Drive, London, N11 3GX
www.mxpublishing.co.uk (UK & Europe)
www.mxpublishing.com (USA)

Thank you to all the women I have had the privilege to meet; who continue to inspire me in my work, and to my family who have enabled me to do a job I love.

In business we must watch and learn, plan and research, consider and re-consider but there comes a time for action. Now is your time for action and, with my help, you can become a successful business woman.

INTRODUCTION

Aged just 19 I embarked on my first ill-conceived business. With a little money from my family, an empty office and a phone, the realisation that business isn't like in the movies hit home pretty quickly. My aims of being a successful business woman faded as fast as my family's belief in me as a business woman.

Since then I have gone on to run both my own and other people's businesses. I now work as a consultant and coach, working with women who wish to be successful in the business world. I have supported many in their dreams to become successful business women. I believe they are all successful in their own way. Some may not have been a success overnight; others had failures before they hit upon the right business idea, while some have gone on to generate success in other areas of their lives.

This book is the book many of my friends, colleagues, associates, clients and I have been looking for in a bid to turn our dreams into reality. A business book which doesn't hide the truth from you and understands the uniqueness of women and the challenges they face when aiming to be "**the successful business woman**".

You may have already purchased and read business books which, while including valuable lessons, are hardly the most interesting or inspiring read. Yes, they tell you the "How to" of setting up a business, yet this is rarely from a female perspective and often fails to touch on some very real issues which need careful attention and consideration before you leave the safety net of employment to start your own business.

You may have been tempted to buy books written by highly successful entrepreneurs who give advice on how you too can be like them. Yet, many of the women I work with tell me they don't want to be like them! Their desires are not to be highly successful multi-millionaire entrepreneurs. Instead they wish for success at some level which considers their personal success targets.

This book will help you identify your personal success targets and help you on your journey in achieving them.

Your business can provide you with the income that you and your family require; it can suit your own lifestyle and play to your strengths. It is my belief that, with a little support, you can achieve the business success you wish to accomplish. It is likely that you already have the ability and determination to set up and run a successful business

This book has been written to provide you with the support you need to turn your business dream into reality.

You may have been dreaming of starting your own business for some time; be it a coffee bar in your local town, an online specialist shop or merely changing the way that you currently work for an employer into a self employed opportunity. Sadly many people continue to dream until they feel it is too late to turn their dreams into reality, considering entrepreneurship as a leap too far. Together we are going to take your dream and turn it into reality now. However long you have had your dream, whatever stage you are at in your life, I believe we can find a way for you to build a business which will suit *you*.

In writing this book I hope to remain true to myself and the work I have done over the years, without simplifying or over complicating the world of business. As such, I promise to avoid jargon, and unattainable business ideals.

The successful business woman's guide shows you how you can start and run a business to suit you and your personal and family needs which will afford you with the right work-life balance and level of success that you hope to achieve. You, like many of the other women I have worked with, can be successful.

When I work with women I look at the following main points:
- Their personal inner strength
- Their desire to succeed
- Their current skillset and core capabilities
- Their business (its concept and operational structure) and how it will work for them.

I believe these points are vital to the success of women in business and, with some good strong business advice added into the mix, business success is possible. Many of the women I work with have no previous experience of business and many have no qualifications; some don't even have a good business idea – they just know that they want to seize control over their working lives and tailor a business to suit their lifestyle and expertise. However, regardless of knowledge, experience or creativity, by considering what I believe to be some key aspects of setting up a business, they become successful business women.

The successful business woman's guide is for anyone who wants to embark on a new way of working and living; as a self employed entrepreneur, and business owner.

Many female business owners I speak to don't see themselves as a business person and would laugh at the suggestion they are entrepreneurs. The reality is I don't actually know what a business person should look like; they are so varied in age, experience, educational attainment, background, and so on. What I can tell you is, like many of the business women I know,

I was hardly what you would consider the "normal business person" myself. That has not stopped me from setting up and running businesses which have been successful for me, my family and my needs.

By deciding to read this book you have already set yourself apart from others. Many people would never consider being in business themselves; they have been conditioned into being an employee. For those people, the thought of self employment or business ownership is totally unrealistic. This is not the case for you as you are already considering earning a living without being answerable to a boss. This book will take you further on your journey to being a business woman in your own right.

Finally, this book aims to help you understand business, how you can set one up and still be a mum, daughter, wife, friend or any other role you have in your busy life. It understands you are an individual and that your individuality must be considered in your business plans.

PLEASE NOTE
The word success is used in this book to mean your own personal level of success rather than one placed upon you by others. Only you can define what success means to you and the level that you wish to achieve. Therefore, when speaking of my own success it relates to my own individual feelings about achieving success and this may not be the same level of success deemed as successful for other people. This book is not about making us all strive for the same levels of success and moulding us all to be the same, rather it strives to help shape you into the successful person you want to be.

This book is based on my views and experiences as a business person and business start up mentor. It is not written to replace the professional advice many new business owners require. Nor is it written as a complete guide to business start up; rather as an overview of how you should approach business start up as a woman. I still recommend that you gain suitable experienced advice from others in relation to your particular business, and we will discuss this during the book.

The stories and experiences related in this book are based on real women's experiences. Some examples have had aspects changed at the request of the individual or to clearly demonstrate a point.

YOU AND YOUR BUSINESS

WHY GO IT ALONE. REASONS FOR STARTING UP
AND THE PROS AND CONS OF BUSINESS
OWNERSHIP

CHAPTER ONE – WHY RUN YOUR OWN BUSINESS?

So here we are together, beginning a journey. I presume you have been considering running a business or becoming self employed for a little while now. Starting a business is something that I believe anyone can do. I'm looking forward to walking you through your business start up from a woman's point of view.

No doubt something has triggered this desire to start your own business. This entrepreneurial spark might be driven by circumstances (losing your job, having a baby, moving to a new area or simply fancying a change) or could be fuelled by something else: maybe a flash of inspiration, a burning long term vision, a passion for something. The women I meet fit into all of these categories and many more. Ultimately your decision may have been born out of passion, necessity or boredom.

For example, my clients give me varied reasons why they decided to go it alone.

Many do so due to changes in their personal circumstances; early retirement, a long career break which has made it difficult for them to return to the same work as before, graduating yet being unable to find suitable employment, or having family commitments and needing a more flexible approach to work.

Others are doing it because they feel there is a better way for them to earn a living; they have become dissatisfied with their current way of working or living and wish to make a more dramatic change than merely finding a new job.

If you are currently dissatisfied with your career, going it alone can reignite the passion and interest you once had in the work you do. It's not always necessary to change both your employment status and specialist area. Sticking to what you know while becoming self employed can be a very positive move for many women who feel there must be something more they can do which harnesses their existing skillset and knowledge base, rather than continuing in their current role.

In general, those who are starting out in business out of choice rather than necessity find the process more enjoyable and fulfilling. Although many report that having circumstances dictate that they review their options gave them the kick they needed to launch forward in setting up their own enterprise. Necessity is often a very good driver and indeed there are those who believe that a business owner who doesn't need the business to be a success, in order to pay the bills say, has less motivation to be a success. Certainly, I believe you need to set our own targets for success and that these will be your personal driver. I will discuss this more as we go through the business start up process in the next few chapters.

WHY OTHER WOMEN DO IT
Your personal motives will be different from other peoples but this makes it no less a reason for going it alone. To help you understand the diversity of reasons why other women started out on their own I would like to introduce you to some inspiring women who we will refer to throughout the book. Each of these examples illustrate how vital it is to tailor your business to suit your own individual needs and motives for starting your own business in the first place.

Lucy is a single mother of three who started up her own Public Relations business because she had the ability to earn a higher wage than she could do being employed. It also gave her the flexibility to be there for her children after school. By selecting her business carefully she has been able to develop a business model which means the hourly rate she is paid is over three times what she could earn as an employee. This has enabled her to leave the benefit trap she found so disheartening and limiting.

Redundancy forced Wendy to reconsider her work and life values. Taking time to consider what was important to her in her life, she developed a food technology consultancy business which she runs part-time and has taken up a part-time position with a local employer. This enables her to continue developing her skills in her specialist field of food technology. Her long-term business strategy is to bring in enough work to pay her the minimal wage required to have the lifestyle she desires. This is enabling her to take the time off needed to build up her small holding where she lives with her parents who she has caring responsibilities for.

After having her second baby, Nicky questioned her reasons for returning to teaching. This and the lack of childcare provision in her town made it difficult for her to return to work. Building up her crèche slowly and with a more educational format than competitors, Nicky has been able to take her children to work with her and continue to use her teaching knowledge and experiences within her own enterprise. Although the path to success has not always been easy, Nicky now enjoys the fruits of her labour with flexible working around the school hours of her delightful daughters.

After 30 years in the clothing industry Joy felt a change was due and, with her children all married and starting their own families, Joy decided her 50th birthday should see her open her own beauty and hairdressing salon. Her experience as a senior manager for a large high street chain gave her the confidence in her own ability but her lack of experience in the sector led to some challenging yet amusing experiences. Her desire to have a different way of working and to have fun at work has kept her focused on how she wants her business to develop.

Clare was made redundant whilst on maternity leave with her son Ryan. Using her redundancy package, savings and a loan, Clare bought the small plumbing firm her brother worked in. Her years in the bank didn't really prepare her for running and managing a busy firm which involved dealing with emergencies, staff, pricing, along with managing vans, stock and the legal side of a plumbing company. However, her knowledge of banking and managing finances has been invaluable. While it was a shame the bank hadn't prepared her for dealing with suppliers, her customer care is impeccable.

WHY DO YOU WANT TO GO IT ALONE?

It is vital that you ask yourself this question: Why do you want to go it alone? You absolutely must explore your personal motivation for starting up your own business. Knowing these reasons will help keep you focused and motivated and assist you in keeping your business in the format you require to suit your lifestyle.

So let's consider for a minute your true reasons for starting your own business. We discussed the potential reasons for going it alone above and you'll learn more about the potential benefits below. They can be major life changing reasons or some simple personal ones. Remember, these are your personal reasons and no one else's. They should be clear to you, to help you focus on why it is you are undertaking this journey. Don't worry about them seeming silly to others, if they are right for you then they are right full stop.

WHY ARE YOU CONTEMPLATING STARTING A BUSINESS?
List the main driving reasons (no more than five) that are making you consider starting a business. (e.g. want a more flexible way of working, like the idea of being your own boss, want to enjoy your work and do something you are passionate about, have a great idea that fills a gap in the market you wish to pursue...)

Looking at the reasons listed above, do they excite you? In other words will they keep you inspired during the intial start up phase and beyond? If not, can you think of other motivators which may maintain your motivation? (For example, the ability to earn a good / better living, chance to develop new skills, opportunities to travel and meet new people...)

Some slightly less positive drivers such as 'I cant find employment' or 'this is my only option' can be worthwhile reasons as well. However, in general I find women need more than that to motivate them on a daily basis. Thinking of things I have already mentioned in this chapter along with your own feelings and considerations, can you now list approximately six reasons why you want this to work for you?

This is great! Well done; it will help us later when we start to develop your business idea.

Essentially though, while your reasons are crucial to help you stay focused and motivated, the key point is that it is your decision. Because, like most things in life, unless it's something you want to do, achieving success will be an up hill struggle. If you want to do this for yourself then the journey of business start up and running your very own business will fill you with pride, enjoyment and fulfilment.

I regularly talk to other women about the benefits of being your own boss. For me and many of the women I know, it has been the most empowering and life changing experience they have had. They often find business ownership opens doors to new experiences and opportunities which they never would have previously had access to. For example these might include experiences such as speaking at business events, travelling, or opportunities to work with more experienced or highly regarded individuals in your profession, maybe you would be interested in the chance to secure positions on pubic body boards and involvement in community development.

I believe in telling people the truth. Sticking to this principle I am happy to share with you the reality of being a business owner, warts and all, so here goes.

THE PROS AND CONS OF BEING YOUR OWN BOSS
PROS
- Gaining Control – To make your own choices and decisions = empowerment
- Flexibility and Balance – Hours, pace, type of work – you decide
- Self-fulfilment, Satisfaction and Pride – You did it! You've launched forth, are going it alone and are succeeding
- Quality of your day - Replace the daily commute, office politics and other employment-related annoyances with time to walk the dog, swim, collect the children, watch TV over lunch and so on

- Making The Most of Your Skills – Utilising what you have to make a real impact is a particularly worthwhile element of business start-up
- The Confidence and The Buzz – Achieving your goals, overcoming obstacles, rising to challenges, developing your business and being truly independent fuels self-confidence and creates a buzz
- Making a Difference – Taking the chance to give something back and to employ others
- The sky's the limit – By removing the employment earnings ceiling you have capacity to earn more

CONS

- Hard Work – It takes a lot of effort to start and sustain your own business
- Increased Responsibility and Pressure – The buck stops with you
- Isolation – No more chatting over your desk (although social networking and real time chat can alleviate this)
- Lack of feedback and support from managers and colleagues
- No employee benefits such as sick pay or holiday pay – you only earn when you work (unless you are able to set up multiple recurring revenue streams)

So let's examine some of these upsides and downsides in more detail:

GAINING CONTROL TO MAKE YOUR OWN CHOICES AND DECISIONS = EMPOWERMENT

Throughout our lives we make many choices: where to live, what to wear, who our friends are, what college to attend, whether to have pizza or curry for tea. However, many women I have met feel that they have little control over some of the biggest decisions in their lives. These decisions are made by their employer or manager. For instance, whether they get a promotion, a pay rise, an opportunity to attend a training course, is all left in the hands of their bosses. Whether they are given time off to deal with family issues, flexible hours to suit childcare requirements, the opportunity to move to a new branch of the firm, those decisions are made by their employers and, even worse, they have no control over if or when they could be made redundant.

For many women the lack of control over what is a large part of their life becomes unbearable. As such, self employment becomes a tempting and often more realistic option than staying as they are. Even when they consider the possible risk of being self employed, it still comes out as a better way of bringing in an income than the more prescriptive employed route.

Working for yourself enables you to make your own choices; this includes the hours you work, where you work and how you work. You will also be able to decide how much you earn, when to take time off and the direction and pace of growth of the business.

In short, women who work for themselves regularly tell me that they enjoy being in control of their own destiny. This empowers them and results in them concentrating more on the job in hand, as previous worries they had at the hands of an employer are no longer a concern they carry with them. They are subsequently more focused and productive which leads to personal growth as they gain confidence as the business develops.

Being your own boss isn't always easy but, in difficult financial climates, at least you know where you stand. If the business is not doing so well you will be the first to know unlike many people who are made redundant and never saw it coming as they are unaware of the financial position of the company they worked for. And, as the owner of the business, by increasing your effort and working harder you have a better chance of earning more money than you would as an employee for a struggling enterprise.

Empowerment. This is an important word to many female business owners. The feeling of control over your own destiny will definitely develop feelings of empowerment and this in turn will help you by building your confidence. Consider this, you will be in control and you will no longer be relying on someone else to decide your fate in relation to a pay rise, promotion, redundancy, recognition, time off or opportunities to work on new projects. Independence, control and empowerment are major benefits to women in particular starting their own enterprises.

FLEXIBILITY AND BALANCE – HOURS, PACE, TYPE OF WORK – YOU DECIDE

I work for myself as do most of my clients; which means we choose our work hours. Consider what hours would suit you and your lifestyle best? Perhaps working only during school hours would best fit into your lifestyle? Or maybe you can only work part time, or evenings and weekends? Perhaps you are happy to work as many hours as is necessary during the start up phase. The choice is yours. Obviously the more effort you put in the more successful you are likely to be.

That said, there is no reason why you can't alter your work hours to fit your personal and business needs. For example, I decided over the last few years to only work while the children are at school. However, if I am busy and there is an interesting project on the go (such as writing this book, for example) I am happy to work the occasional evening. Having the flexibility to put in extra effort when workload dictates is necessary, but this goes both ways, as you can take time off during less busy periods and make your working hours work for you and your lifestyle.

Taking the dog for a walk in the middle of day becomes a way of getting a break from your desk or some fresh air, occasional long lunches with family and friends, a lunchtime swim or whatever else you would like to be able to do can now become a reality, without the need to feel guilty. It is all about working out a timetable which suits you and your business. Essentially, balance becomes more attainable when you are your own boss.

How do you feel about having more control over day-to-day and long term decisions about how, when and where you earn your income? I suggest you now start considering some of the decisions you would like to be able to make about the way you wish to live and work. Becoming self employed will not only change the way in which you work and earn a living, but it will also affect the way in which you live your life. So take some time to consider what these changes will be and how they will impact each area of your life. We will explore in Chapter Two the importance that the choices you make regarding how, when and why you work for yourself have on your lifestyle.

HOW WILL YOU WORK?
What time of the day do you work best? (e.g. morning)

What hours are difficult for you to work? (e.g.weekends)

How many hours would you feel happy working in an average week? (Please be realistic)

Do you want to be able to take breaks during working hours? (e.g. going to the gym when it is quiet).

Where would you prefer to work? (e.g. from home, in an office with others, or varied places if you like change)

The answers you have provided above about how you will work will become more relevant as we go through the business start up process. We'll be examining in more detail the hours you work and the location you choose to work from in Chapter Two. It's important not to forget these when you start up your business. Ask any business person and they will tell you that you can all too easily get wrapped up in the business and forget some of the original reasons why you started up your own business in the first place.

During this initial start up phase you need to start being in control of how you want your business to work for you. Too many business people I meet are working for their business and, to be honest, they may as well be employed by someone else. What I mean by this is that you need to make sure your business works for you as much as you work for the business. One of the big benefits of being your own boss is having the freedom to decide things for yourself about the way in which you work, so you should take advantage of that freedom. Furthermore, by having to initially wear all the hats (admin, consultant, tea girl, PR, distribution, accountant...) it's easy to get caught up working *in* the business rather than *on* the business. But sometimes you will need to step back to work on the business strategy and planning rather than on the day-to-day workload and administration.

I once spoke to a female business owner who, after many years of business ownership, had made a big change in the way she worked. Standing at Euston station together she explained to me that, after a series of nannies and au-pairs and the high cost of childcare, she had decided that enough was enough and she may as well take advantage of the flexibility being the boss gave her. She now takes the entire school holidays off and has designed her business so that it works perfectly well without her during school holiday time when she spends time with her four children. She told me "Getting away from the business works well; we all benefit from it - for me, the family and the business".

It hadn't always been this way for her, initially she set up the business with a male colleague and it wasn't until she bought him out of the business that she made the changes which now make her feel more in control. "I do still need help with the children after school and if they are ill," she says. "But, I now look forward to my time with the children and I also enjoy my time in the office with a great team, who, to be honest, enable me to have the lifestyle that I wanted."

This story isn't that unique. Many of the women business owners I work with take time off to suit their family requirements, whether that's caring for children, grandchildren or an elderly relative. They either put the business on hold or have staff that can run the business for them in their absence. Having clarity around what you specifically want from the beginning will enable you to set up the business to suit your needs. I used to do much the same when the children were younger, reducing my hours or not working at all in the school holidays.

You will however, need to be realistic about how flexible your particular business will be. Some businesses are simply not flexible, such as a shop with 9-5 and Saturday opening hours or a pub open until late at night. You will need to identify in these cases whether you will be able to manage the hours required or if you will need some help, when that help will be needed and how much that will cost you.

Very occasionally I meet people who have started their own business and aren't able to enjoy the flexibility it could bring. They have such an intense workload that they can't take time out, find the lack of structure hard to handle and need to enforce some framework to enable them to reach their potential. I regularly hear employed people say things like "I couldn't work for myself I'm not disciplined enough" or "I couldn't work from home because I would sit watching the telly all day in my pj's". Well, first of all, if you really want to be a success you will have to learn to motivate yourself and be disciplined. The reality is, if you don't get the work done you only have yourself to blame. Secondly if you don't work and put the effort in you will soon have no money, now that is a great motivator.

It is therefore a good idea to set your working hours (whether they are: 9-3, 10-5 or 5-9) and keep to them. Personally I get dressed ready to go to work, take the children to school and on my return from the school run go straight into my office. Once I have started the day it seems much easier to keep going. I know others who get up, go for a run and shower, dress in work clothes and go to the spare bedroom office by eight in the morning. Discipline pays dividends as your business will benefit. More control, flexibility and balance may be key benefits to starting your own business but, once you have decided what suits you, I recommend you stick to it.

- Create structure. While flexibility is a useful benefit, running a business takes effort. Make sure you set clear hours, put in the time and delegate if necessary.
- Consider your personal needs and family responsibilities. How can you fit your business to suit these? Use the opportunity to a) suit your lifestyle and give you some balance and flexibility and b) make changes in your life.
- Consider what other changes you could make to your life now that you are enjoying more flexibility?

For example, working for yourself is a life changing experience in itself, but it also provides you with the opportunity to make additional changes to your life. I'm not suggesting anything dramatic, as starting out on your own will be time consuming and needs lots of energy and focus.

What I mean here is that there may be things about your life now you might like to alter; things that, by having this more flexible way of working, are now realistic.

For instance, perhaps you have always wanted a dog, but being out at work all day has prevented this. Or maybe you wish to reduce your carbon footprint by getting rid of your car. These and other things may now be feasible. I know many people who started exercising more regularly when they started their own business, not only because they could, but also because they felt it was important to be physically and mentally fit and healthy in order to give everything they could to their new business venture. For me, working from home has in the past allowed me the freedom to run a family smallholding, keep animals and grow vegetables for the family. I don't have the smallholding anymore as I now run a B&B as well as doing consultancy, but growing vegetables and my animals continue to give me a contrast from work which I enjoy and benefit from.

Clearly, there are a plethora of benefits that running your own business provides, from control and fulfilment to flexibility and change. Let's examine some additional plus points about going it alone.

ADDITIONAL BENEFITS OF BEING A BUSINESS OWNER

SELF-FULFILMENT, SATISFACTION AND PRIDE
The satisfaction 'you did it' is a vital driver and beneficial feeling for business owners. There are many milestones during the lifetime of your business when you will swell with pride knowing that you have done it for yourself. Some women have told me that such satisfying back-patting moments include: the launch of a new product or business, articles in the paper about you and your business achievements, seeing others enjoying your products, (especially watching someone walk past in one of your outfits) hearing someone complement your business not knowing that it's you who owns it, getting customers coming to you because someone else recommended them, seeing your name above the shop door,

17

taking your first pay packet, paying someone else for the first time and seeing your products on the shelves of a major supermarket.

Each of these milestones fuels your passion as an entrepreneur to continue to drive the business forward as you witness how the harder you work on your business, the more rewards you reap. Such feelings of achievement mean a lot more than any pat on the back that you might get from a manager or employer, because you did it yourself – *you* made it happen!

MAKING THE MOST OF YOUR SKILLS
Fulfilment and pride. Many people in employment feel that their skills are not used to their full potential in their current workplace. Being in business will enable you to use all the skills you currently have and develop many more. You will also be surprised at just how many skills you actually have already which are beneficial to business. Fundamentally, you will never feel underutilised again.

THE CONFIDENCE AND THE BUZZ FROM RISING TO CHALLENGES AND DEVELOPING YOUR BUSINESS
Facing challenges. Day-to-day challenges will present themselves and keep you busy. They will keep your brain engaged and active. Many business owners believe that these obstacles are what excites them about being in business. In essence, rising to face the challenges makes them feel alive and provides them with the drive to continue. Remember, in business you will face challenges (call them 'challenges' rather than problems or difficulties) which you can overcome and learn from. Furthermore, successful entrepreneurs know that learning is a key ingredient of success. A mistake is only a mistake if you fail to learn from it. As such mistakes and challenges are vital learning tools in a business woman's armoury.

The buzz. Speaking to a fellow business owner once at a conference we both admitted to having an addiction to the buzz that being in business gave us. Like me, she had been in business many years but had kept that buzz alive by continuing to adapt and develop her business to maintain her interest in it. I too adapt and develop my business to give me variety in life the same as an employed person might go for promotion or a new job. Finding what gives you a buzz will help you keep fresh and alive as a business owner for years to come. While the confidence gained from reaching targets, rising to challenges and overcoming obstacles increases that buzz.

MAKING A DIFFERENCE

Many business owners make a difference directly through their business, either giving a percentage of their profits to charity, allowing staff in their business to give time and services free to local charities and community groups, or by offering services to disadvantaged groups at reasonable rates. Other business owners tell me that, because they can control their working hours, they are able to give time to local and national organisations that they wouldn't have been able to had they been employed.

For many business owners being able to make a difference is important to them and, as such, they consider the impact they might be able to have on their local or global communities and environment during their start-up phase. You could consider setting the business up as a social enterprise or running a business which enables others to access something they wouldn't usually be able to.

The new skills and confidence you will develop in starting up your own business will become useful to organisations you may wish to support. Many women business owners have used their knowledge and skills in business to help start up community initiatives. For them, giving something back helps them to retain important links to the community and balance their lives.

NEGATIVE ELEMENTS OF WORKING FOR YOURSELF

As with most things in life, working for yourself is not a bed of roses. Indeed, there are some aspects of starting up your own business which are not so pleasurable. It's up to you to consider if the positive sides of being your own boss outweigh the negatives; for most women in business they do. If they didn't then they wouldn't continue to run their own businesses year after year. Some of the less pleasurable elements of entrepreneurship include:

HARD WORK TO BUILD THE BUSINESS

It is usual to expect the start up phase of any new business to be hard work. This doesn't necessarily mean you have to work excessive hours. Some women decide to start up their business part-time initially in order to juggle other areas of life, maintain a part-time employed position and essentially test the viability of their business in action. Others accept that the start up phase will take longer as they can not or do not wish to put in excessive hours Some women decide to work whatever hours it takes to start and get their business out there in to the market place as quickly as possible, only taking time out once it is successfully running. There is no right or wrong way. However, the upside of working hard is that you and you alone gain the benefits of your hard work and not some fat cat employer. Remember you are doing this for yourself; to contribute something valuable and worthwhile for you and your family's future.

ISOLATION AND LACK OF FEEDBACK AND SUPPORT

If you like to receive regular feedback and praise about your work, think carefully about how you will gain this. Whilst it is true that, without a boss, you are unlikely to get regular structured feedback, you can often get feedback from others.

Yet there are often times when you have little or no feedback about your work or maybe only negative feedback. Consider how this will make you feel and how you will manage this. You may feel happier having a structure in place to gain feedback, in the shape of a business partner, business advisor, mentor or coach. It's worth speaking to other business owners about these options so you can get such support in place early on. Isolation from colleagues can also be tough if you work from home as you have little or no face to face interaction. However, there are forums, social and business networks and chat technologies that can alleviate such isolation.

INCREASED RESPONSIBILITY AND PRESSURE

The buck really does stop with you; there are no excuses if things go wrong. You may thrive on having this higher level of responsibility or may find it difficult to get used to. If taking full responsibility is going to be too much for you, consider getting a partner for your business or running a franchise with support from franchisees. I've watched many women who had previously felt overwhelmed by the potential responsibility of being a business owner, only to see them actually thrive on this new level of responsibility as this business develops and grows.

THE RISK ELEMENT

Setting up your own business is a risk in itself. That's why it's crucial to prepare yourself as much as possible in order to de-risk the process of stepping away from job security. Business owners often take risks throughout the lifecycle of their business; the level of risks you choose to take will depend on you, your business and your personal circumstances. In general, research has shown us that women take less financial risk in business than men. If risk is something that concerns you, be aware of this during your business planning stage. It is not actually necessary to take big risks and many business owners take little or no risks for the life of their business, preferring to err on the side of caution and play it safe. While it is true that often, in business, the bigger the risk, the bigger the reward, there is no point putting everything on the line without diligently accessing the risks involved to make informed decisions going forward. As such, I believe that successful business owners take only calculated risks and the level of risk required will all depend on your business idea.

THE FIRST RISK-ASSESSMENT: IS BUSINESS START UP REALLY A GOOD IDEA FOR YOU?

It is natural for you to have some doubts about your ability to run a business. You may be concerned that you don't have the relevant skills and experience to succeed. Whilst we will examine the skills that will set you in good stead, it is important to get all negative thoughts out of your head right now so that you can properly assess the risks of going it alone.

You see, many successful business people had little or no experience before they started up on their own. In addition, many business people have little or no formal qualifications and many have admitted to low levels of numerical and literacy skills. Whilst I feel you need some basic level of these skills, the reality of business is that you can develop a business that suits your own skills and levels of ability and learn other skills as you go. You can also employ people with the skills in which you are lacking.

Some women are concerned about how others will view them in their new role as a business owner. Possibility this is born out of their own negative experiences of business people they have met, or the way business people, particularly business women, have been portrayed in the media. It is possible that people will view you differently as a business owner, but most women tell me that this is a positive experience as many people congratulate them on having the drive and ambition to do it for themselves. In general you are likely to inspire other people if you go it alone.

One of my key secrets to success is keeping true to your own values and morals. We will examine this later, but, on the whole women tell me running a business has only changed them for the better. They believe it develops the real person within them. Whilst some people may have a perception of entrepreneurs as the ducking and diving Del Trotter or ruthless Ian Beale, most realise that real business ownership is nothing like it is portrayed on the television and they begin to see the work you need to put in to be a success in business.

HOW TO MAKE THE MOST OF BENEFITS AND REDUCE THE NEGATIVE IMPACT OF STARTING YOUR OWN BUSINESS:

- Get a coach or mentor to help provide you with feedback and support you, acting as a sounding board for you to bounce ideas around with and discuss ways of tackling challenges.
- Sign up to a networking group which has face to face meetings and an online forum so you can discuss ideas, seek advice and post questions to gather feedback from like-minded individuals.
- Consider timing – is now the right time to start your business? Are you prepared or able to work hard to start and sustain a business of your own? Do you have too much going on in your life currently to add to the pressure with the responsibility of entrepreneurship?

LEAVING THE EMPLOYED CULTURE

Leaving the employed culture behind is rarely difficult for new business owners, and once they have made the decision to step out alone they don't look back at their old 9-5 life. However, I do find that some women who have been involved in the mad corporate culture for many years before going it alone, find it difficult to adjust initially. They start off working as they had intended, hours to suit them, not taking on too much, but soon slip back into the same long hours, unrealistic deadlines type culture they had been trying to escape.

While some new businesses do take a lot of hard work and long hours to get going, it is important to fit them around your lifestyle and what's important to you. In the next chapter we will begin to discuss this in more detail and will review why you wish to leave the current working life you have. It's easy to replicate what you are trying to escape, so it's important to remember why this move was important to you and put systems in place to avoid falling into old habits. Consider keeping time logs to really understand how much time things take as we regularly miscalculate the real amount of time that tasks require.

It may be difficult for you to make a clean break from being employed in order to start up on your own. Maybe you need some financial security from an employer, at least part-time, to keep paying the bills while you launch forth with your new venture. This is not uncommon, with more and more people running their business after they have done a full day at work. This part-time 5-9pm business format enables you to try business ownership without leaving the security of the day job. However, if you have other commitments, you'll need to address how you can maintain balance while working in the evenings on your business. However, working part time for an employer and part time in your business can be tiring.

There are many other half way house possibilities though, such as going freelance and maybe even starting with some work from your current employer. Many individuals go freelance, carrying out services such as marketing, PR, training or other specialist support for companies on a retainer basis, and many maintain a relationship with their previous employer who may agree to hire them for a few days per week, giving them a secure income stream whilst building up their additional client base.

Naturally, leaving what seems like the relative safety of employment, to take a gamble on self employment is a major step for anyone. The reality is, at some point you will have to take a leap of faith, but please don't do this until you have done your homework and planning. The following chapters of this book should make the transition from employment to self employment a much happier and less risky one.

BUSINESS START-UP AND YOUR LIFESTYLE

You need to really spend time thinking about your own needs and how these will need to be considered in your business planning. Think about your personal commitments, family, childcare, financial etc. Think also about planning for school holidays, personal development, moving from your current situation, (i.e. employed, stay at home mum moving into self employment).

As outlined at the start of this chapter, for many of the women I work with lifestyle reasons, such as greater independence and control, factor highly in their motivation to move into self-employment. The way in which you live your life and the way in which you could be earning your income will have a significant impact on the lifestyle choices you are able to make.

The next chapter will help you to select the business you wish to run to suit the lifestyle you wish to have. Being clear about this from the beginning will help you to develop a business model to suit you and your needs. This is where we can really think about you and building your business.

REVIEW OF CHAPTER ONE

- Do start considering your personal drivers which have led you to consider running your own business.

- Don't have negative thoughts about your ability to run a business.

- Do consider the pros and cons of starting your own business and how you can make the most of the advantages and minimise the disadvantages.

- Do think about making choices for you in line with your needs. Consider the bigger picture – does the type of business you intend to start up fit with the hours you are able to commit to it and therefore will it provide you with the balance and lifestyle you want? Ultimately will you be able to make the most of the flexibility and balance that starting your own business can provide? (We'll tackle this in detail in the next chapter)

- Do start speaking to other women in business and asking them their reasons behind business start up.

- Do keep positive, you will soon be considering a big lifestyle change which could be the most positive and life changing thing you have probably ever done.

CHAPTER TWO – DEVELOP A BUSINESS TO SUIT YOU AND YOUR LIFE

Let's take a little time now to think about you. What type of person are you? What keeps you interested, motivated and gives you that buzz? What are you good at? What makes you happy? The easiest way to answer such questions is to recall things we have done in the past which have inspired us. For instance, arranging a fundraising event or managing plans for your wedding or a big holiday abroad may have given you that buzz. Maybe you have felt particularly inspired at work when developing a new product or putting a new team together. Whatever it is, keep it in mind while we consider exactly what you want from your business. Running a business is hard work so it is critical that you enjoy it; that you feel passionate and motivated enough to drive the business forward even during tough times.

It is possible to make some silly mistakes as you are swept along with the excitement of starting your own business. Most surprisingly, often the biggest mistake I find is around the appropriateness of the business for you. For instance, I once met a lady who had set up an online baby shop where she would have no contact with customers, yet she admitted to being a people person and found being at home all day with little human contact was making her very unhappy. Had she gone through the exercise we are about to do, and asked herself what kind of person she was and what made her happy at work, she wouldn't have started up such a venture in the first place, or she would have at least tweaked her business idea to ensure it involved some contact with others. Similarly, I knew an artist who took space in a studio with other artists but found the constant chatter and people coming in and out a distraction to her and her work. It would have been far more appropriate for her to work on her own, possibly from home.

Think now about what you need from your business to keep you personally happy. Do you relish working alone or with others? Do you prefer working indoors or out, enjoy variety or routine? Working for yourself enables you to make choices about the way you work. That's one of the clear benefits to most business women I know, so you should certainly take advantage of that freedom to choose a business and method of working that makes you happy, motivates you and makes the most of what you are good at. So let's now map out some of the elements which make you the unique person you are.

What are you good at? (For example, you might be particularly good at: organisation, financial planning, getting on with people, etc)	What makes or did make you happy at work? (This might include: being with others, helping others, learning new things, variety, getting out and about, and so on)
What skills do you have? (Your main competencies might include: craft work, cooking, teaching, selling, communicating, designing, writing, and so on)	What knowledge do you have? (You might have knowledge about a sector or information that few people know about, such as technical knowledge or industry-specific expertise)

WHAT DO YOU WANT?

What success will look like for you will partially be determined by what you do and don't want from your lifestyle. Maybe you don't want to have to travel and be away from home or maybe you don't want the responsibility of staff. Lots of business owners don't do it for the money but for a more balanced lifestyle. An example is the owner of a B&B' who only opens part of the year, earning her enough money so she and her partner can spend three months in the sun over winter.

It is worth listing some of the things you do and don't want as a result of running your business so that you can consider them during your business development stage.

What I don't want	What I do want
e.g. to work weekends	e.g. flexibility and some time to myself

You may want recognition, money, more time off, respect from others, or flexibility from your business. These and so much more are all possible if you plan, work hard and consider how you will achieve them (but more about that in the planning chapter).

Take some time now to evaluate your responses above. Can you now see that there are some things which make you happy and confident which you must consider when you are developing your business? For example, if you have said you like variety and being out and about, being locked away in an office five days a week is not likely to motivate you. Conversely you are likely to feel miserable. This is a simple exercise that so many budding entrepreneurs forget to carry out as they rush headlong into their new venture, and yet it is so crucial to evaluate these areas, so that you end up doing something that you are confidently competent at, making the most of your skills and expertise, in a working environment that makes you happy.

WHAT BUSINESS HOURS WILL YOU BE ABLE TO KEEP?

While we consider how to ensure that your business fits your lifestyle, it's important to consider the hours you feel able to put into your business from the outset. Be realistic about the hours you will be able to work, considering everything else you still need and want to do in your life and also the hours that will be needed to make your business a success.

For instance, let's say you're teaching piano lessons and the hourly rate in your area is £20. If you need to earn £300 a week, you will need to work a minimum of 15 hours a week, that's without considering any costs for advertising, materials, tax or insurance. You might be planning on only working Monday until Thursday. What's more, your customers are primarily children after school, so you may only able to teach from 4pm. You would need to average four pupils a night meaning you would be working until 8pm. Do these hours suit you? And how realistic do you think it is to get four pupils, four evenings a week, every week of the year, summer and winter?

We will examine how to generate custom in more detail later on, for now lets concentrate on the hours. After all, as outlined in Chapter One, control and flexibility around the hours you work is a key reason for starting a business of your own. As such the hours you work needs vital consideration. It's true to say that you tend to get out what you put in. There are only a few exceptions where people work very low hours and get paid very well, especially during the start up phase of their business.

HONEST HOURS

Consider the fact that, if you only work a few hours, it will take you a long time to get your business built up. Your business may not be as successful as you wanted it to be and customers may become frustrated that they can never get hold of you or they have to wait too long for the product or service to be delivered.

However if you work too many hours your family and friends may get fed up that they never see you. You may become fed up with the business as it is taking up too much of your time. Also I believe that answering e-mails at two in the morning can make customers think that you're not in control and can't cope. You will also find that, if the majority of your time is spent on the business, you will not be getting time to rejuvenate.

As a busy woman, whether you are a mother or not, you are no doubt already aware that time management is a fine art. It can be difficult to get the balance right when starting your own business – you need to work hard and put in the time and effort to get it off the ground and sustain its growth, but you may have started the business to give you more flexibility and improved work-life balance, so you don't want to have less time with your family as a result, or your reality may be at odds with your reasons for starting your own business. Clever planning of working hours is therefore key. Often you'll need to make sacrifices (usually when it comes to me-time) at least initially, until you can afford to employ help.

Many women I work with, who are now working more hours than they ever did during their employed existence, need to be reminded that one of the reasons they went into business in the first place was to have more time for their family, for hobbies or for themselves. Of course many people understand and accept that they will need to work excessive hours to build up the business rapidly, at least at first. The long-term aim being to take time out once the business is established. Anyone entering into self-employment must be prepared to work long hours to launch the business, however, it's important to be careful not to fall into the trap that so many new entrepreneurs fall into; i.e. of working unreasonable hours and never reviewing if self-employment is really giving them what they want.

If you feel that you can't give many hours to your business, consider whether you are ready for self employment. Whilst I believe you can make your business flexible, running a business will take up time and requires commitment and a large dose of persistence. As mentioned earlier, you could consider other alternatives, maybe running it part-time, going freelance, working with a partner or working for another small business to see the way they do it and discover if that suits you.

Ultimately, this is *your* business and you can build it how you want. Either by putting in extensive hours in the first few months before becoming more flexible later on or benefiting from the flexibility that your business can provide from the outset to suit the needs of your life and family. For example, having run my own business since the age of 19, when the children were young I rarely worked during July and August as the children were at home. It tended to be a quiet time of the year in any case, with many clients taking holidays. I took advantage of this and I didn't take on any projects during this time, ensuring that I completed any ongoing work during June.

I still kept in contact with e-mails and enquiries but nothing major. Clients knew this and were happy to wait if necessary.

As long as people are kept in the loop they understand that everyone needs to take time off. We all need a break to recharge our batteries; it's good for us. Indeed, when you're employed you would get annual leave.

Times have changed for me now and my children are growing fast and so I have been able to adapt my working life once again to my needs and those around me. My daughter leaving home and her brother entering high school has given me more flexibility with the types of work I take on and new business ventures I become involved with. As our life as a family changes so does my business, and this can happen for you too. That's the beauty of the flexibility that running a business brings. As a small business owner you are nimble, adaptable, flexible.

Naturally, deciding your working hours based around holidays, pursuing your own interests and lifestyle choices, is a key benefit of working for yourself. The vital consideration is to ensure that all stakeholders in your business (customers, suppliers, staff, and so on) are aware of your working hours and that you (and they) know how you will be able to leave the business should you need to go away or are unable to work for any period of time.

Fitting your business into your already busy life can sometimes be a bit of a challenge. Remember Lucy, the single mother of three who started her own PR agency? When she established her business, she knew she would only be able to work during school hours and occasionally in the evening when the children had gone to bed. She also knew that this would mean she had to select projects which wouldn't require her to travel far or to regularly work evenings. Lucy was realistic that some days the children would be ill and that the holidays would need to be planned like a military operation.

However, her determination to be there for her children kept her focused on building a business that would work for her and her family. As the children have grown up, so too has her business as has her ability to take on a wider variety of projects. Being honest with clients about deadlines and setting realistic work levels keeps Lucy level headed and in control of her business, rather than the business controlling her.

- Consider the hours of business your potential customers might expect you to be open.
- Consider which hours a) you are at your best in terms of creativity and productivity and b) suit your lifestyle and personal needs.
- Be realistic about how many hours you can actually do, both in the short term and in the long term. What type of help will you need to keep to these hours? And how will you ensure the business is providing quality service even when you're not there?
- Ensure honesty. Whether you decide to run the business part time, or only at the weekends, work school hours or only evenings; ensure that people will have the same professional experience whenever they approach your business. If your advert or sign on the door says you are open from 10-3 then make sure you are open; a hand written note saying "sorry popped out" can be more than a little irritating to a potential client.
- Communicate. Let customers, prospects, staff and suppliers know if you need to take a break or make any changes to your existing hours.
- Be prepared. Flexibility works both ways. While it affords you with time off to perform tasks that you need to do,

you may have to take on additional responsibility or have back-up plans, for example if childcare arrangements collapse.

Although Joy had no direct childcare responsibilities when she opened her salon, her daughter would often ask Joy to help out with her granddaughter. Joy tells of one occasion where, in the middle of a packed salon, her granddaughter began screaming. Unable to pacify her and deal with the customers simultaneously, Joy gave her granddaughter a pen and note pad to entertain her. This worked for a while. But what a shame it was the appointments book that next drew her granddaughter's eye! Joy and her staff spent the next month's having to write appointments in over crayon scribbles and smeared biscuit, hardly professional.

HOW MUCH INCOME DO YOU NEED?

Diligent preparation is one of the most important aspects of starting a business of your own, not only when it comes to what you put in to the business, but also when it comes to what you take out of it.

Be realistic about your ability to earn enough money from the outset. All businesses take a little time to establish and build up. Taking a wage out of a start-up business can be difficult in the first few months. You need to ensure that you will be able to pay your bills and live as well as affording costs of running and promoting the business. I recommend saving up enough money before you start to keep you going for a minimum of six months. It's reasonable to think that you will be able to take some money out after that point, all being well.

- Consider what you actually need. List all your expenses honestly. How much do you really spend each week? List

36

everything you would need to pay out over a 12 month period. This will include insurances, Christmas and birthday gifts, mortgage payments or rent, household bills, shopping, clothing, petrol, car maintenance and tax, gym membership fees, nursery fees, magazine subscriptions and so on. Also allow for those one off bills like repairs to the washing machine, new tyres or your cars MOT. Total it all up. Gulp! (I know, it's always more than you think).

- Figure out how much will you need to spend on your business, both in terms of initial start-up expenses (stock, website, business cards and tools to help you) and ongoing running costs (rent, stationery, printer cartridges, salaries, tax and so on)?

- Take advantage of the many online tools or software available to help you to calculate your personal expenses and consider areas of saving.

- Review those living expenses realistically. Look for things you can cut back on, such as coffees with friends, satellite channels that you never watch or consider reviewing suppliers of gas, telephone and other utilities to save some of your hard earned cash.

- Seek out additional ways of generating income. I know lots of people who rent out a spare room in their house, do some occasional temping work, or declutter and sell their second-hand goods on eBay or at car boot sales, to bring in a little cash to keep them going during business start up. As mentioned earlier, starting your business part-time while retaining a part-time job or evening work may be viable.

- Consider the effect the change in your income and outgoings may have on your family. Will they have to go without things for a little while? How long will that be and how fair is that? Discuss the reality of the situation with your partner and whether they can support you during your business start up and, if so, for how long. It's best to agree things in principle to ensure you both feel there is an element of control over the situation.

- Estimate when you are most likely to start generating income from the business itself and how so. Budget accordingly. If you are planning to live off savings for a while make yourself a sensible budget and work out how long it will realistically last before you will need to take money out of the business.

No one said this was going to be easy. This is a vital part of your planning process. Remember what we have already discussed about making this business fit around your needs.

KEEP CLEAR DISTINCTIONS BETWEEN BUSINESS AND YOUR OWN LIFE

It's all too easy when you work for yourself to blur the boundaries between your personal home life and your business, particularly if you work from home. A business friend of mine told me that business provided her with a heady mix of work and family, that she believed you needed to concentrate on only one at any one time. She found that, even if that is 30 minutes for the family and 30 minutes for the business, it was by having boundaries and keeping them separate that she found neither the family or the business suffers and she can maintain some level of sanity.

Clare ran her 24 /7 plumbing businesses from home with a hotline into her family lounge. The phone constantly rang and, whilst she was dealing with other peoples emergencies, mini crises would erupt in her own home, whilst her ever growing brood of children were left to their own devices. Friends and family began to feel awkward about visiting in case she was busy, and her relationship with her partner began to break down. It became clear that while it was one thing for the business to be a massive part of her life, for Clare it had become almost the only thing in her life. With help and support we turned her business around and she now uses an external firm to manage her out-of-hours calls and pass them on to her staff to handle. Her children have their mum back to help with homework and after school activities and her partner and family are happy to have her back to relative normality.

When PR agency owner Lucy started running her business from home she was on the phone to a potential big client when her baby, sat in the baby chair next to her desk, filled his nappy. She had two options: 1) try to finish the call as quickly as possible and then change baby or tell the customer "I have to go, baby has filled his nappy." Just think how I felt when she told me she had done the latter! Oh dear!

In another incident Lucy's six year old son proudly told one of her big corporate clients that she was in the toilet and couldn't come to the phone. When asked if he could call back shortly her son replied, 'she's locked the door so she could be a little while.' Maintaining a high level of professionalism at all times is crucial in business, another reason to create distinct work-based boundaries within the home and vice versa.

Similarly, when my son was young he ran into my office to tell me he had done his own shoe laces. This was a big moment for us and luckily I had an understanding client on the phone at the time who knew I was a working mum. However, this led to the rule in the house that 'if mummy is on her work phone you mustn't speak across her.' My children have been known to pass me notes and use sign language to let me know what they are doing. I don't think this has harmed them in anyway (it has, however, helped them to develop their creative communication skills) and they understand the importance of customers to my business and have learnt that it is possible to wait five minutes sometimes.

When it comes to the telephone, don't let the kids answer it or anyone else who will give a less than professional image. Be organised and ready for when the phone rings, have a pad and pen by the phone, as there is nothing worse than listening to someone scrabbling around for a pen when you are trying to discuss business with them. They may laugh but what are they really thinking?

If you're not able to ensure your telephone is going to be answered professionally consider an answering service. You can outsource both the handling of your phone calls and other secretarial duties to a virtual assistant.

Be realistic about how you will work and live and keep clear boundaries between the two, with 'no business here' zones across every area of your life and 'do not disturb' parameters during working hours. Even your wardrobe is likely to be divided into formal work and informal home clothes.

Have 'no business' times of day as well as 'zones'. For example there are some days I don't have my mobile switched on. Taking time away from the business to do things with friends or family often means you will return to the business with a new perspective and re-established vigour. Having friends who are in no way linked to your business, whom you never talk about the business with, affords you with the priceless opportunity to relax and be yourself. Indeed, this becomes increasingly important as your business grows.

Despite creating no business zones, there will be some areas of overlap. Indeed if you are running a busy business from home there will be some inevitable impact on the family home, no matter how organised you think you are; from business paperwork and supplies strewn about, to the home phone line tied up with work calls, clients visiting and so on.

The key to minimise disruption to family and work is to keep everyone informed about the rules, boundaries, plans, events and so on. Consider the impact it may have on your neighbours, you and your family, with additional comings and goings or increased noise. Inform your family and friends about your new way of life. They should be aware that you are implementing some major changes and what this means to them. Hopefully this will give them the opportunity to see how they will be able to support you to achieve this new stage of your life.

How will your business impact on your daily life? When I was young, my mum worked from home making stuffed toys. Many tea times were spent sat amongst teddy bears and rag dolls, with evenings spent stuffing legs and arms ready for her to make up the next day. It didn't do us any harm (in fact it inspired me in a way) but I'm sure sometimes my parents felt like the house was being invaded by toys.

As such, it's worth establishing some boundaries and rules. :
- Let family know your working hours so they can avoid them unless it's an emergency. Ban people from popping in for coffee during working hours if you're working from home. People wouldn't do it if you were at work elsewhere, so the same rule needs to often apply. At our house, friends and family only visit after the kids are home from school as that's when I tend to stop for the day. Just because I am at home doesn't mean I'm free and available for a coffee and a chat. Gently remind them you are actually working, as many people forget. You'll be amazed by the amount of people who don't consider this.

- Keep personal phone calls to a minimum too. If you're with a customer, you hardly want your best friend to call about her latest love-life disaster. I find setting some parameters works, such as asking friends to only call me after 12 noon or to try to call me in the evenings.
- Consider how you might deal with enquiries outside of your normal working hours
- Focus on your business and on your life... SEPARATELY. Do not mix the two up. We all need some down-time where we are free from business dealings and likewise time to focus on our business, undisturbed.
- If you can have a second phone line installed for the business or only use your mobile to receive business calls it can make it easier to ensure the phone is always answered professionally.

YOUR BUSINESS LOCATION AND YOU

The topic of maintaining clear boundaries between work and home leads to the important question of where you will run your business from. You will need to decide whether you require business premises or not. If you're planning on running a shop or a business where customers need to come to you on a regular basis, business premises are likely to be a must. Yet many businesses in the UK are run from home very successfully. Running your business from home will provide you with more flexibility in your working hours and you may find it easier to arrange work around your caring responsibilities or other personal needs.

Clearly where you will run this business from will have an impact on many areas: on costs, family life, your well-being. Choosing the right location is key. Many women I work with start running their business from home; some see this only as a temporary measure as they plan to grow their business and take on suitable business premises in the future; others expect they will always run the business from home. Alternatively some businesses require premises from the very beginning.

HOME RUN BUSINESSES

Working from home really works for some people. They like the flexibility and work-life balance it provides, the lower cost and financial risk in establishing the business plus the lack of travelling required. Others tell me they find it lonely and difficult to motivate themselves into setting a routine and keeping to it.

Consider the following:
- Keep set business hours
- Create your own work space and keep everything for the business in one designated room of the house or use a separate building such as a shed, converted garage or garden office. This could be the spare bedroom, a converted attic, the garages or shed. Google and eBay began life in their founders' garages and many of my clients run successful businesses from garden sheds, outhouses and lofts.
- Ensure you have space to store your work things even if that is just boxes in a corner or a cupboard.
- Establish some way of having some human contact, ideally with other business owners and those with similar interests to yourself. Business networks may be a good place to start. Alternatively I know women who get their human contact from joining a sports club or painting class; whatever works for you, just make sure you do get out and about at least a few times a week to avoid the cabin fever that can suppress some entrepreneurs.
- Stay motivated by setting yourself some ground rules about how and when you will be working. Experience tells me that planning the week ahead and setting targets and rewards for yourself works. While it can be tempting to have a lie in, work in your pyjamas, sit with a laptop on a

comfy sofa or get distracted by the TV, I find that, in order to stay motivated and focused it's best to get up as if you were going to work outside of the home, dress reasonably smart, have breakfast, clear away and then get to work. Discipline is critical. If you don't put the effort in you won't be paid. It's as simple as that.

Whatever you decide; make it work for you. Remember what you decided early on in this book about your desires to develop a business which suited you and your needs. Don't be over distracted by the lure of business premises before you really need them, they may look good but can you really afford them? They will certainly eat into your revenues.

There may be some legal issues in using your home to run your business, depending on the business and the type of activities carried out there. It may also affect your mortgage and home insurance. You may also become liable to pay business rates. Seek professional advice before you start trading from your kitchen table or spare room. Some home businesses will have to have specific planning permission. Check with your local council.

I used to work from our spare bedroom until my son was born and then I moved into the study, which I shared with the rest of the family. Sharing a study didn't work for me so I opted to move my work away from home, taking an office on a business park for my team and I for many years. More recently I have changed the business and I now work from home again, as it suits me to do so at this time. I find it's best to do whatever suits you, your business strategy and those around you at any given time, even if that means making some changes to the business.

Business owners who work from home talk about needing to be able to escape from it all, otherwise they feel like they are

44

constantly at work. I work from 9 – 12, take a lunch break and eat a proper lunch then work for another few hours. I generally take a break, then go for a walk or get some fresh air and a change of scene by popping out for the paper. I can always go back to my desk and work for a while longer if I feel the need. The point is that it's wise to take a break and get a change of scenery if you work from home; another reason why setting clear physical boundaries is so important – to distinguish areas for work from areas for living, relaxing and socialising.

TAKING PREMISES

If you're taking a work space away from home there is a lot more to consider. We will talk about the cost in more detail during you financial planning. For now, let's consider if the shop, warehouse or office you are considering is going to work for you. Is the atmosphere right for you? Will you be able to work there to your best in terms of productivity? For example, I know of women who set up their first businesses over chip shops or on industrial parks. These locations were hardly inspiring but it's all they could afford. I do understand that, however, we are trying to make this business something you feel happy with and content to run. The location of the business will really impact on how you feel about going to work every day.

Taking premises can eat into much needed cash resources which is why many people avoid doing so until their business outgrows their home office. However, some businesses need premises from day one.

If you decide to take premises, shop about for good deals and the right location. Don't make the mistake of going for a cheaper out of town location without considering the extra you will need to spend to get people to find you. Signage, adverts or PR can all add up so that your cheaper rent doesn't look so cheap anymore. Consider all consequences that each potential location brings with it.

Be realistic about how much premises will really cost you. It's not just about rent. What about the rates, electricity and telephone? Does it need furnishing or decorating? You also need to look at the terms of any lease or sale of business premises: what are you getting for your money? What extras might you be faced with? If you're renting, what deposit is required and when will the rent be paid? Fundamentally, are the premises suitable for your business plans? If you need to break out of the lease agreement, how easy will that be? Will you need to gain a change of use from the council? How will other business owners feel about your business opening next to theirs and vice versa?

You may also like to consider flexible business premises solutions. Many towns and cities now have office spaces which are available on a flexible basis. Smaller offices within larger premises can be hired at fixed monthly costs allowing you to plan for the expenses. Alternatively, serviced offices are another viable option for some small businesses which provide you with more than an empty shell, including furniture, IT support and even a receptionist to answer calls and take messages. These will often have meeting rooms on site which you can hire out as needed to avoid paying rent on an empty meeting room.

Many small businesses use virtual offices, which can handle their mail and manage telephone calls, whilst also providing the appearance that you have a professional office while you may actually be working from home. This can be a solution it you don't want to use your home address on your business documents and wish to convey a professional image by having a city based address. Ask the local council if they have incubator units or speak to a large firm who may have space they are willing to lease to you.

Instead of taking on a shop for selling your goods, consider whether you could sell on a market stall or at events and country fairs. The overall cost of the stall hire and pitch fees are likely to be lower and more flexible than a permanent site such as a shop.

Be careful not to go for the first available option. Look around for a solution which best suits your needs (both current and future) and those of your customers.

Once you have decided on your business premises, be it a shop or office, get someone with experience in business leases or sales to help you through the process, to check the paperwork and help you secure the best deal. Sorting out your business premises is a big step in starting your business, it can be the key to your success. Ask for help to ensure you get it right.

When Lucy started her business she worked from home, but with a small house and three busy children to accommodate, running the business from the table in the corner of the living room soon became unbearable. She couldn't afford the rent of an office nor did she want any big commitment, Lucy was thrilled when one of her clients offered her a small office in their building for a basic monthly rent.

It worked well initially for Lucy, however soon the client became more demanding of her time, popping in when they felt like it and making it difficult for Lucy to give equal time and attention to her other clients. Lucy decided it was time to leave when she overhead the Managing Director talking to visitors in the hall way telling them that Lucy was their PR Manager and making out she was a full time member of staff. Lucy left soon after and had a lovely and particularly un-shed like garden office built. Subsequently she now has the best of both worlds: a personal space to work in whilst still being at home.

Whether you decide to work from home, from a purpose built office in the garden or take premises, ensure your work place is a comfortable place to be. Believe me you will spend many hours there so you may as well make it nice for you. Things don't have to cost much to ensure you have a great working space for your new business.

Meetings at Home
Consider whether it is wise to set up meetings in your home. Think about your safety as well as the image it portrays. If you want your image to be a home based friendly service, that's fine. However, not all customers will be happy to meet you sat amongst the trappings of your family life. It can be a bit too personal. Many a time I have been to someone's home for a meeting to be sat next to a smelly dog, remains of last nights tea in the sink or, on one occasion, a baby lamb sat under the desk! (Don't ask!)

The alternative is to meet clients at their premises or hire a meeting space for these occasions. Many places now offer meeting rooms by the hour or day at reasonable rates. It's also becoming more acceptable in some businesses to meet in the coffee shop near their office or a hotel bar.

You may have to re-evaluate working from home as your business grows and expands. Consider aspects such as storage of stock, admin and paperwork. If you need to have staff will you be happy to have them come into your home, or could your first few members of staff work elsewhere, possibly from their own home? As your business grows you may need to get more business space without moving out of your home. You could consider a garden office or an extension at this time.

TRAVEL

Some business sectors require regular travel. It's important to consider the impact this will have on your life, your family, your pets and your health. Is this the new way of life you have been planning or does travel not suit your dream? Be clear about what times and in which circumstances you are prepared to travel. If someone then calls and asks you to attend a meeting at the other end of the country, you will be ready with your response because you have already decided what you will and won't accept as reasonable.

There is more to travelling than the time and the cost. When Joy needed to travel to promotional events she would worry about the security of her home and her personal security returning home late at night to an empty house. It wasn't something she had done before. She decided to find a solution to her safety concerns by fitting lights, alarms and using a reputable taxi firm rather than change her business plans.

Consider how you might use technologies as an alternative to travel. Video conferencing technologies, such as Skype, have come of age, while real time messaging such as Microsoft Messenger and other web based meeting solutions can enable you to have conversations other than over the phone.

WHAT ELSE IS GOING ON IN YOUR LIFE AND HOW WILL THAT IMPACT ON THE BUSINESS?

We've taken some time to review the business side of things in terms of location, hours and so on. Now it's time to refocus on *you* again. Think for a few minutes about what is going on in your life and how they may impact your business dreams.

From the arrival of a new family member or future plans to have a family, to moving to a new area, ageing parents or other dependents requiring care. Perhaps these responsibilities will increase during the next few years. Will you be able to cope with these responsibilities and build a business?

Clare took over the plumbing company when her son was at full time nursery. The cost of the nursery ate into the little profit Clare was making during the early stages of her business ownership. Once little Ryan began school the cost decreased, but the hassle increased. Nursery had been open 8-6 and school was only 9-3; the school holidays seemed to come around quickly and, with little family support, Clare had to re-plan her business to enable her to manage this new way of life. As her family grew Clare adapted her business by taking on part time staff to cover some hours and being more systematic with her work to enable her to take more time off out of term time.

The beauty of running a small business is that your enterprise is far more agile and nimble than large corporate counterparts. You can adapt your business to your ever changing life as long as you set it up in such a way that you are able to do so; shrinking, growing and shifting your business to suit you and your responsibilities as and when necessary. As long as customers see little effect on the products they purchase and the service they receive, you will be surprised how adaptable many businesses can be.

YOU AND YOUR HEALTH
Keeping yourself fit and healthy is an important part of being self employed. If you are unable to work due to poor health how will the business carry on without you? And, if you have staff, will they know how to manage? Apart from having

manuals and plans in place to ensure others are easily able to step up to the mark, you should make sure you take care of yourself. Eating healthy and only snacking on brain food (nuts, seeds, fruit and so on) are all important, especially if you are working from home and can access the kitchen at any time. I learned early on that stopping to eat a proper meal was never wasted time. Equally, getting as much good quality sleep as possible is also important.

Many self employed people will tell you that you must look after yourself. An unhealthy person is less likely to be reliable for customers and, as a self-employed person, if you are not well enough to work, it's more than likely that you will not be earning. Sick pay is generally a benefit that only employed people earn.

I strongly recommend having a back up plan if you're ill or you need to take time off to care for a family member who is sick. What I have learned is that you're nearly always struck down with something when the business is at its busiest, or when you're needed to attend an important meeting or you have an unrealistic deadline to meet.

You'll be pleased to hear that taking time to rejuvenate yourself, with a few days off, a holiday or some personal pampering time can boost your creativity and productivity levels. See getting your hair done or a massage not as a special treat but an essential part of your business success! Perfect.

THE EFFECT OF BUSINESS OWNERSHIP ON YOUR ROLE AS A MUM
If you are a mum, consider the effect business ownership will have on your role as a parent. This can be positive and negative. The positives, such as being able to take children to from school, attend school sports days and such like, will make up for the times you can't be there for them.

Lucy developed her business model so she could be there for the kids. She set the times of the day to suit their school hours and only having appointments with clients during those times. Inevitably there are times she can't be there for the children, but she believes it has had a beneficial effect on her relationship with them. She is now there for them more often than not. And, on the odd occasion she needs to be away from them, they hardly notice she isn't there. Lucy does need to consider the cost of occasional childcare, but the peace of mind it provides outweighs the costs.

If you believe you are doing this for the benefit of your children and to support your family, consider if they actually want this to be the case. You really will need them on your side some days. I have often had to explain to the children who are bored during school holidays that we can't go out today as mum has work to do for a client. In those instances I remind them that on other days we get the benefit of me being at home and they usually understand (well that and some form of bribery often helps). Starting up a business without the support of your family can be very tough indeed. I have watched many women struggle with balancing family and business. Don't let this happen to you.

The good news is: my children and the children of many of my clients have told me what amazing and inspirational role models their mums have been for them. Additionally you will be pleased to know that children of enterprising parents are more likely to be successful business people in the future. My mum always had some money making plan on the go when we were kids. Helping her stuff and wrap bears and make labels in the run up to Christmas was great fun and no doubt paid for my new bike that Christmas. Kids need good role models and what better for them than seeing mum become successful, happy and confident. As long as that is the result that running a business is having on them. Children don't want to see a mum who is over stretched and utterly stressed.

With that in mind, you will need help sometimes. Consider then how you will manage early morning starts, late nights and evening events, time away or illness. Try to develop a support network around you. As you know, when my children were young I would take most of the summer off to be with them; it was only six weeks a year. During that period I would slow down the work and work only evenings and weekends, when their dad was around to help out. This also meant I could help my full time working friends with their children during the holidays. I could often ask them to return the favour during the school term when I was stuck. More recently as the children have grown things have changed and I now have a second business in tourism so we tend to be busy in the summer, when the children can now pitch in.

ARE YOU REALLY SUPERWOMAN?
It's not that likely that you and superman are best friends. I learned very quickly that I wasn't superwoman; the outfit wouldn't really work for me anyway. Seriously though, please accept that you can't do everything and, if you try to, you can make yourself ill. By taking time to consider what you need to put in place to enable you to run and grow your business organically rather than manically, is time well spent. It is likely that you will need some occasional help. So, if someone offers their help, accept it. Don't see it as a failure on your part, you have nothing to prove. A great thing about the world of entrepreneurship is that people love giving advice. While people may not always be generous with discounts or giving things away, they are more than happy to be generous with the advice they give. Seize that opportunity to learn from others, who can fill the gaps in your knowledge or skills base.

We will talk again about how to best make use of people's help in the business, but for now it's enough to consider that you can ask others for help. While women in general are often inspirational, nobody's perfect. As women we are great at multitasking, but you do need to be realistic about what you can take on. Don't be like one of my clients who would call me on her hands-free kit while doing the dishes and all I could here was flying pots and pans; or the lady who would call me while out on her morning run; heavy breathing and business discussions don't tend to mix! Remember to remain professional at all times, right from the beginning. This is one of my key principles to business success that I teach time and time again.

Review of Chapter Two

- Start now to think about what you want from life and your business. It must suit you and your needs from the outset. It must be appropriate to make you happy and fit your lifestyle.

- Think seriously about the hours you can work and how you will manage. Be realistic about how many hours you can actually do, set realistic work levels and be honest with clients about deadlines.

- Talk to your family and friends about the way running a business will or possibly won't impact on them and you.

- Be realistic about how much income you need. Be prepared. Save enough money to keep you going for six months. We will need to reflect on that again during your business development stage of the book.

- Accept you are not superwoman, even if you are an amazing woman. Accept help and develop a support network around you.

- Keep distinguished boundaries between your work and life. Set parameters regarding when is acceptable to call/visit.

- Take care of yourself. Sleep well, eat well, give yourself some me-time and fresh air.

CHAPTER THREE - YOUR VALUE SYSTEM

Values are the beliefs and feelings we express and live by in everything we do. The values you hold will be deeply held beliefs about what is right and wrong, good and bad. These are your core values, which are often in line with your family values. Certainly, for many of us, our values are developed during childhood, often passed down to us by our parents or those who've had a significant impact on our lives. Our values can be adapted and built upon as we journey through different stages in our lives and encounter different experiences.

You may not regularly consider your values, but they will impact the decisions you make, actions you take and the way you behave in society. I believe these values should be considered when you start up your business to ensure you feel comfortable with your enterprise, its purpose and what it essentially stands for.

WHAT ARE YOUR OWN VALUES?

Consider for a minute your own values about the way you live; the way you behave, the way you interact with people or how you wish to be seen by others. Now consider their importance and why they are so important to you.

Note your values here:

Most people have the same basic principles as others whom they come into contact with; from the way they behave in business, and the level of respect they show for each other, to the words they deem to be unacceptable in a business environment or their views on trust and transparency.

Consider what others might feel about your values? Will you expect them to consider and understand your values? Are some of your values a little extreme or out of the ordinary? Will other people find it difficult to accept or relate to your values? You may feel it is important for you and your team to have fun at work and feel relaxed, and as such you might decide to encourage the wearing of casual clothes, jeans and t-shirts. You and your team may feel comfortable with this, however will all your clients?

Remember Joy who started her beauty salon at 50? Joy had strongly-held values of respect for others. She felt that the principle values she held about respecting other people's privacy, belongings and rights would hold her in good stead as a business owner. Difficulties arose when Joy recruited several younger staff members into the salon. Although they also had respect for others, it was not to the level Joy expected from her team. Joy had to learn to understand that different generations will adopt different values or levels of values, while trying also to instil her values into her team in terms of what she expected from them.

WHY SHOULD YOU CONSIDER YOUR OWN VALUES IN BUSINESS?
Starting up in business is a big step and some days you will need to dig deep into your reserves of confidence and determination to overcome obstacles. The last thing you need is to have doubts about the integrity of your business. It's

therefore vital that you feel comfortable about yourself and your business, and the way that both are conducted.

If you feel your business is in line with your morals, values and beliefs you will believe in your business. Having this belief in the business; knowing that it is fundamentally good and you are providing a great product or service to your customers, will make selling to those customers a much easier and more comfortable experience.

Ultimately, your value system will help underpin your mission statement and your purpose. If you believe in treating people as you wish to be treated, being open and honest and being punctual, you will likely have a mission and purpose to give your customers the best possible quality and reliable service.

Over the years I have had vast experience of selling to customers, either within my own business or someone else's. During my time as a mature student, I took a part time job at the local estate agents. Until that time I felt selling was simply selling and that I could sell most things. What I hadn't bargained for was my values getting in the way of commission. I hate the idea of taking advantage of vulnerable people so, when showing an old lady around a house not suitable for her needs, I realised quickly trying to sell to her wasn't an option for me. I did try the rehearsed patter but simply couldn't do it. My values got in the way. We quickly mutually agreed the house wasn't for her and left. The upside of this story is that I sold her a bungalow a few weeks later which suited her needs perfectly. She could see that I had morals and values and consequentially trusted me to find her the house she really needed. That gave me the edge over competing agents.

THE IMPACT OF BELIEF
If you believe in your business and the products you are selling, others are more likely to believe in them too, both the staff

you employ and the customers you sell to. Much of being a business owner is getting others to trust you and want to do business with you. They want to know that you feel accountable for the products you are offering and believe that they are the best you can offer. Belief in your business begets credibility which boosts sales. It's as simple as that.

Take Nicky and her crèche. Knowing she trusts her own children to be cared for in the crèche even on days she isn't there, goes a long way to reassure other mums who feel able to trust the care of their children to the crèche. Additionally, when Nicky speaks of the crèche, her passion for quality provision and education shines through and makes you feel comfortable that she knows what she is doing and that maintaining a high standard of quality is one of her core values.

Essentially, if you feel positive about your business and strongly believe it is a good company then you will sound more genuine, caring and confident about your business when you present your offerings to other people. Most of us would rather buy from a business owner we believe we can trust and who is passionate about their business

KEEPING IN LINE WITH YOUR VALUES, BELIEFS AND MORALS
By keeping in line with your personal values, beliefs and morals your level of integrity will show through in the way you run your business, not only for customers, but suppliers, staff and competitors. In general, all businesses have competitors, and the ones I worry about are those who have integrity and are based on foundations of good values and strong morals. I never worry about the ones whose scruples are somewhat doubtful, as they usually don't last long.

Furthermore, getting others to work with you is much easier when your values are clear and your team are on-board with them. Most of us would rather be linked to people with similar values to us so, as an employee or a business partner, we tend to ensure that people's morals and values are in line with our own. Alignment of values will avoid future difficulties when we are asked to do something which we feel uncomfortable with. Having clarity of purpose with clear values makes it easier to create a culture of like-minded people who are striving for the same goals in the same way; a genuine team with aligned morals and a united vision and mission.

Wendy, our food technology consultant, was offered an opportunity to be involved in a project which would see her visiting potential customers and sharing with them the benefits of a particular product. She was offered high levels of rewards for doing this, yet she wasn't convinced the product was value for money. She called me because she was worried that if she were to demonstrate this product to her customers, they would then link her to this more expensive and inferior product. Their trust in her would diminish. "Have you ever used this product in your business?" I asked her. "No," she said. "I have the less expensive more modern one."

I asked her what the problem with the product was? She explained it was out of date and the newer product that she used was cheaper and better quality. I asked her why she didn't sell that product then, the one she actually used and thus believed in? But Wendy explained that it wasn't sold through agents and they were not known for the hard sell. We then discussed what makes her money and she said giving consultancy advice. "That's it then isn't it?" I said to her, "you don't feel comfortable selling product x and anyway you make your money giving advice, so don't sell the product and you can recommend to clients the one you would buy. That way they trust you." In the world of consultancy, trust begets loyalty and loyalty begets referrals and repeat custom.

Wendy continues to use this principle as a business owner when deciding what she will and will not become involved with. She often speaks about it with other business owners saying how simple it is to become distracted by money making opportunities. But she knows her values and core business mean she must believe in something before she asks her own clients to believe in it. As such her values underpin her business strategy decisions.

How Your Values Will Benefit Joint Working and Cross Selling

Many business people have close links with other business owners. We will talk again about building these links, but for now let's consider how your values and those you place in your business will affect partnerships.

There are three key ways of benefiting from strong links to and partnerships with other business owners:

1. **Boosting sales and/or adding new revenue streams.** If someone likes and believes in your product, they may be happy to sell it along side their own, usually for a percentage cut. This is not the same as being a supplier; these are one off deals.

    Joy upsells in her beauty salon. Several local small

business owners leave their jewellery products in a display cabinet in her waiting area. If she sells anything on their behalf she receives a 10% commission of the price. It's not much, but Joy likes to feel part of the business community, it adds to her revenue, and the items cheer up her waiting area. She only selects quality items that she feels comfortable being linked with her business.

2. **Generating referrals.** We are all much happier to recommend someone with similar values to ourselves. Many business people rely on others recommending them. Much of my business over the years has come from word of mouth recommendations from previous clients or business connections who know they can trust me. On the whole we find it difficult to recommend someone we wouldn't trust ourselves. If someone asks about a local garage they can use, you will tell them which ones not to go to because you don't trust them. You only recommend those who you can trust to do a good job. If someone is merely acceptable, you probably won't recommend them. This is because we don't want to recommend someone and then discover that they did a poor job. So you would rather recommend someone you have complete faith in rather than someone who is mediocre. Hence the importance of having strong values to build trust and integrity while also delivering on expectations.

A good example of mutual recommendation is Lucy. As a PR consultant and advisor she often gets asked to be involved in the launch of a new product. She is happy to do this, but doesn't have the staff or expertise to do the event management work. She works closely with another company who does and is happy to recommend them to clients. In return,

*the event management company recommend her
when people need PR. "I feel happy recommending
each other in this way " says Lucy "because I know
the owner has very strong work ethics, she also
values her customers as much as I do; no money
changes hands, we just do reciprocal promotion of
each other and mutually benefit from that".*

3. **Improving your value proposition.** Forming partnerships
    can be a very strong way of developing your product and
    adding value to your existing offer. Lucy does this by
    working with other agencies. Alone, she may not always
    win larger projects, but together with another company,
    she can form a good team. Currently Lucy only
    recommends the other company, but she could form a
    stronger partnership where they bid or quote for work
    together, filling the gaps in each other's areas of
    expertise, and price themselves as a complete package.

*Similarly Wendy could work with a photographer or
advertising company that works with food
companies. Together they could price up full
projects for consultancy and marketing of new
products. These could enable her to win and work
on larger projects, but as part of a bigger team. This
could also help her with her future strategy as well
as stopping her feeling so isolated when always
working alone.*

CONSIDERING SOME COMMON VALUES
Staying true to your value system makes you and your business
ethical. However, there's another set of values that can make
your enterprise even more ethical - Corporate Social
Responsibility (CSR). As a business purpose, CSR is becoming

increasingly popular. In short, it is a way in which large organisations take responsibility for the impact their organisation has on communities, the environment and the people it comes into contact with. This takes the organisation beyond the statutory requirements placed upon them and gives additional attention to being involved and making a difference in a voluntary capacity. For example, a factory might support the local school by giving them a new mini bus or an estate agent may sponsor the local football team's strip.

Whilst I appreciate your business will not be a large corporate body (well not this week) you may still like to consider the impact your business will have on others. Is there a way you can offset your environmental impact so that others see you as a more positively involved and responsible business?

Take Nicky, for example. In her crèche she only allows children to have cloth nappies. She has done a deal with the local nappy laundry company who collect the nappies from her. In fact, the parents leave all their nappies there to be collected so the laundry company lowers its carbon footprint by not collecting the nappies from individual homes. It also means it's easier for the parents all-round.

Additionally Nicky buys her food produce locally and, where possible, chooses organic and free range. She takes the impact of her business seriously and tries to encourage recycling and car sharing amongst staff. She also gets involved in fundraising for the local community. In general her community see her business as a big part of the community and, in turn, they support Nicky where they can, even turning a blind eye to the extra traffic and double parking during the morning drop off period.

BEING A GREENER COMPANY

Nicky is also keen to do her bit for the environment. It's not that difficult to consider the environmental impact of your business and it needn't cost you the earth (excuse the pun). Indeed, such environmental consideration often saves you money. I am a keen recycler. Being kind to the environment is one of my own personal values which feeds into my business. As a result, paper in the office is recycled with confidential material being shredded and used as bedding for our chickens and ducks before being composted; it's a great way for dealing with secure data.

Recycling and reducing fuel consumption are some considerations, but you could go one step further and strive to reduce your business's entire carbon footprint. Some things such as reducing your travel are easy to do, particularly if you're planning on working from home. Using technology, a little common sense and some planning ahead can help you and your company be that little bit greener.

You may wish to take it a bit further and promise to offset your carbon emissions by planting trees. Just consider what your customers will think of you. How will the perception of your business as environmentally friendly impact the brand you are building? Will your environmental values align with theirs? People are becoming more aware of environmental issues and, as a responsible business owner, so should you.

BRANDING

Branding is about so much more than just the name of your business. It is about your purpose and values set. Your logo, graphical elements and the colours you use are all about personifying your business by giving it a personality, by bringing it to life.

What are your brand values? How do your personal values and business values translate into your brand? Are your customers likely to relate to those brand values? For example, if customer care and support is important to you, can this be shown in the brand values, brand name, logo, strap line or maybe a customer charter or promise?

Positioning your business well with the current trends, desires and values of your customers can be make or break for your business. You may be making a new cheese from your organic milk produced on your farm and using organic locally sourced products. Using these elements in your branding and putting the customers' experience at the heart of what you do could be the difference between a contract with a major supermarket or having the hard slog of visiting farmers markets and small shops to sell your product.

THINK: DOES YOUR BRAND MAKE OTHERS WANT TO BE ASSOCIATED WITH YOU?
When it comes to your logo, the colours you choose and the words you use to define and emblemise your brand and its values:

- Consider drafting a design of your logo and then hiring a professional designer (or a friend who is good at design) to do it for you. This can be worth the investment if the brand and image it portrays is important to you and your business.
- Consider whether your logo can be seen as clearly in black and white as in colour on your web site, adverts, printed products, and packaging.
- Spend time thinking about strong strap lines, key words and phrases to link in with the brand personality. It's important that the words and graphics you use clearly

convey your brand values, whether that is providing value for money or high quality, or promoting a way of life. Think about "Tesco – every little helps" or "Nike – just do it".

- Be careful that your strap line doesn't constrain your businesses future growth and development. "Amy's Hair- for stylish hair in your own home" may seem ideal now while you just do hair, but you may wish to diversify and offer make-overs, nails or wedding packages in the future, in which case you will need to modify your name or strap line, a potentially expensive exercise, especially if you've invested in signage.
- Use clear statements and messages in your branding materials and be consistent... **always!** Clever words or phrases which need explaining can get lost or misunderstood. **Keep it simple!** Keeping 'on brand' in all your communications is important. Small and new businesses often let themselves down by giving mixed and often confusing signals.

| **What look and feel are you trying to achieve?** |
| Start to consider the words you would use to describe your business. Note them down below. |

| **Now re-visit the words you have noted above and consider how you can change these words to show your true brand and personal values.** |

| **Consider words that refer to quality, value, excellence, flexibility, uniqueness and other positive brand images.** |

CONSIDER WHAT IMAGE YOUR BUSINESS PORTRAYS
Branding and values are about perception and how others perceive you and relate to you. Another consideration therefore is the image you portray in terms of how professional you appear to be. i.e. Do you build confidence in customers and potential customers or do they worry that you will not be able to deliver what you have promised? While you should be honest with people, it can damage the professional image of your business if you tell people you've only just started or that you don't have proper offices yet. There is no need to lie to customers but do they really need to know that you're running the business from the spare room or kitchen table and that you have to fight your teenager for the home PC to check your e-mails? Always consider the image you are portraying.

It is possible to portray an image of confidence and ability and make your business appear bigger than it really is. Perception is important. Some home-run one-woman-bands go one step further by getting virtual offices (if necessary) in other parts of the country or even the world, simply to convey an image of being a larger and therefore credible organisation.

When Wendy talks to clients she doesn't let them know that she still works part time for a law firm. They don't need to know that she can't speak to them on a Monday or Tuesday because she works for someone else those days, just as clients don't need to know that you only work on the days when your child is at nursery. Wendy tells clients its best to call her later in the week or that she only makes appointments on Wednesdays, Thursdays and Fridays. She is honest with them but doesn't reveal everything and therefore retains a professional image.

Speak to your potential client group about their values. Ask them to tell you what is important to them both in general and when they are buying your type of product or service. Either speak to them directly or carry out on-line surveys to help you answer questions like:

- How important is cost to you when buying xyz product?
- Rank the following in importance when purchasing xyz, price, safety, quality, brand, location, etc
- When considering your purchase of xyz how much do you consider the environment?

Using the above as examples come up with your own questions below.

Now consider who you could speak to in order to get some feedback about these areas and how will you incorporate their views into your branding.

Much of the way in which you portray your image is down to choice; you need to decide to portray yourself as a serious business woman and your business as a solid business. Being professional and behaving in a professional way will help to ensure that others take you seriously. Being punctual for meetings, dressing appropriately and appearing organised all help in building trust in you and your business by conveying a credible image.

I often hear non experienced business women saying things like "I can't come Tuesday as I'm taking the baby for her injections," or "I don't have the car on a Wednesday as my husband needs it." A client does not really need to know this extra information and relaying it gives the impression that you are not in control.

One of my pet hates is women using handbags in meetings. I regularly see women rooting in their handbag for a pen or their business card or worse, a mobile phone which is playing some inappropriate tune. Arrive at meetings organised and at least appear in control. Keep your work things together; use a folder or briefcase to hold note pads, pens, business cards and information packs. A handbag is fine for your keys and bits and bobs but keep your work things neat and together to save the embarrassment and awkwardness of rooting in a bottomless pit for a scrunched up business card.

Things don't always run smoothly in our house, with pets, children and all the joys they bring. But telling a client how difficult my morning has been getting the kids to school or dealing with some near disaster isn't usually a good start to a meeting. Arrive on time, organised and ready for business.

You are representing your brand. Think how professional you come across; how others view you and your business. Take yourself seriously; it will help others to do the same.

REVIEW OF CHAPTER THREE

- Accept you have values which are important to you. Stay true to them in business in order to feel comfortable running your business, remain credible and enable customers and staff to relate to you and your purpose.

- Believe in what you stand for and in what you offer. When you believe in your business, so will others. It's easier to sell to others who feel you value and believe in your products and services.

- Consider how your value system might impact your business by helping you to improve your offering, add extra income streams and generate referrals and loyalty from customers. Consider how your value system might impact others: your community, environment and so on.

- Consider having environmental and /or socially responsible values in your business.

- Understand that others also have their own values and be respectful of them even if they differ from yours.

- Does your brand make others want to be associated with you? Are your values and messages clear, concise and consistent?

- Consider how you are representing your brand by what you say and do and how you appear in meetings. What image do you and your brand portray?

- Consider partnering with like-minded people and businesses to earn commission, generate referrals and cross-promote.

CHAPTER FOUR – YOUR SKILLS, EXPERTISE & CHARACTERISTICS

The best businesses make the most of the owner's individual skills, areas of expertise and personal uniqueness. Certainly, running your own business will be your opportunity to make use of all your skills and even learn some new ones. For many women, running their own business enables them to make use of skills for the first time which have previously been ignored by employers.

I am often asked what qualifications and skills you need to run a business. There is no definitive answer to this question. Many business people have few or no qualifications including the likes of Sir Richard Branson, however it depends on your business. For some professions you need to be relevantly qualified to perform the services that your business provides. For example, if you are setting up as a mobile chiropodist I hope you are a qualified chiropodist. Some trades don't require formal qualifications but having them can help boost credibility, such as being an interior designer. Many businesses though require no qualifications and you certainly do not need a qualification in business studies to start your own enterprise.

Clare's confidence was knocked when she was made redundant. With a new baby and a new business her life had changed dramatically. It was so important to build her confidence so that it didn't affect her business plans. Clare and I spent a lot of time considering her skills and the value she could bring to the business. Not only did it help her regain confidence in her own abilities but also to focus on what areas she could work on in the business and what areas she needed support with. Clare found by concentrating on her skills such as organisation, financial planning and motivating other she could develop a business which suited her strengths.

As the business grew so did Clare's confidence in herself. She soon began to attend networking groups for other business women and this in turn helped her grow and develop as a person and as a business woman; all from reviewing what skills she had and utilising them. Clare explained later that this had always been a frustration for her when working in the bank as she knew her skills were underutilised and she felt undervalued. Now she worked for herself she had control over the use of her skills and always tries to remember this method of reviewing and harnessing skills when it comes to her own staff.

Skills and experience, on the other hand, are a bit different. All business owners need skills in some area. I know you will have some skills which will help you set up and run your business. So let's review your areas of expertise and discover what you can do already.

Make a list of five things you have done well in the last two weeks. Be specific; rather than just writing 'I worked on Monday and Tuesday', say 'I did everything last Monday and Tuesday that I planned to do and also developed an action plan for my business'

Make a list of five qualities or skills you have. Be specific; rather than writing, 'I am good with my hands' write 'I am creative and make items of craft to a high standard' or 'I am good at prioritising and getting things done in the order of their importance.'

List five achievements from your life so far. Again be specific rather than writing. 'Getting a degree' consider 'achieving my degree even when faced with obstacles and knowing how to use what I have learnt in my day to day working life'

Avoid using negative assumptions about your abilities or qualities. It may be strange to be writing positive things about yourself however, when you have an urge to qualify a comment about yourself by using words such as: 'fairly well', 'quite often', stop and turn those into positive statements. By spending time on a regular basis reviewing what you have achieved it will provide you with a more positive and confident

74

outlook. We spend too much time reprimanding ourselves for not achieving or not finishing something. Instead of going over what still needs to be done at the end of your day review what you have achieved in order to finish on a more positive note

It's no good being modest here; these skills will pave the path to your future success. The more aware you are now of your skills and abilities, and the more you consider what you enjoy doing and the experiences you can draw on, the easier the business planning will become and the more enjoyment you will get from running your business. Everyone likes doing things they are good at. Furthermore, by outlining your skills and strengths you will also find it easier to see what skills you are missing and any areas of weakness, which is helpful when it comes to hiring staff who have those skills and / or developing your own skills.

WHAT ARE YOU GOOD AT?
Consider the following:

Transferable skills - You may have skills which can easily be transferred to a business. For example, the ability to balance the household accounts will help you understand accounts in the business. If you can teach the young people at the youth club about yoga, maybe you will be good at explaining things to people, pitching to clients or working with young people.

Qualifications – While you may not necessarily need qualifications, it may be that previous qualifications gained could help you in your business more than you realise. So list them as well.

Specific Skills - Write down job related skills you have like managing staff, developing new products, planning events or writing proposals.

What previous work skills do you have? (e.g. managing staff, handling money, handling customers, using a computer, writing adverts.)	What experiences can you draw on? (e.g. working in the hospitality industry, being part of a large company, experience of working in politics.)
What skills do you have from your personal life? (e.g. managing the household budget, being diplomatic, ability to get on with people, ability to drive, organisational skills, etc.)	Of all of your skills, which do you enjoy using most? (e.g. being creative, helping others, writing, problem solving, leading a team, playing an instrument, presenting to a group, etc.)

After filling in the boxes above, review them again in a day or so when you may feel differently or when you have had time to think, filling in any gaps as you go. You could then ask a close friend, colleague or family member to go through this exercise with you. They may help you to be less critical and reveal areas in which you have skills that you'd not even considered.

WHAT SKILLS AND QUALITIES DO YOU NEED TO RUN A BUSINESS?

While you should ideally be skilled and experienced in the sector in which you intend to start a business in, not all business owners are. For example, many people set up their own restaurants having no previous experience in the hospitality trade; however, they may have worked in retail or in marketing and therefore have some relevant skills that may set them in good stead, such as good people and planning skills.

Similarly, while someone may have no experience in a particular area they may have the qualities you need to be an entrepreneur. For instance, they might have a strong desire to learn, be persistent, determined, flexible and energetic. So you see, it is not only about skillsets and experience, your personal qualities, your attitude and seemingly non-relevant skills also come in to play.

Nicky has always come across as confident and knowledgeable. Nicky says that the parents who use her nursery say this has helped them when selecting a nursery for their children. It is important in her sector for the customers to feel the environment provided is safe, professional and of a high standard. Nicky says she feels confident that her nursery and the staff she employs are able to provide this and she is therefore confident when she speaks to parents. I can also say that it is Nicky's communication style which is professional yet relaxed and homely which adds to her obvious knowledge and skills base which probably comes across when parents talk to her.

All entrepreneurs start their first ever business with no experience of running their own business. They may have learned a little from working in a family-run business, or working in another small company but have never actually been responsible for establishing and setting up their own enterprise until they do it the first time. So you're in good company.

As such, if you have no experience of running your own business and want to boost your confidence before launching forth, there are training courses you can attend regarding business start up. These can vary from a few hours or days to several weeks of training. You will need to decide whether you need (or want) this type of training. Reading a book, such as *The Small Business Start-Up Workbook* in addition to the one you are currently reading, may be all the business training you need. Lots of people benefit from a short 'business start up' programme which may help them concentrate their efforts and consider new aspects as well as learn about the support on offer in their area. It can also be a place to meet and connect with other budding business owners to gain some mutual support.

The company who look after my online business presence started up in business the same month as I did. The owner and I met on a business start up programme (Ok, it's going back a long time now). While the programme wasn't particularly helpful, we have always kept in touch and still do business together and seek advice from each other.

When it comes to running your own business, while you should take time to read books such as this one and prepare, you will learn the best lessons by actually getting on and doing it. That can-do attitude – of taking action – is one of the key characteristics that entrepreneurs should have. There are many people who dream of setting up a business of their own, but only a small proportion actually do it.

Other key elements I feel you need to be a successful entrepreneur are a willingness to:
- Work hard
- Learn
- Take careful and calculated risks
- Lead a team
- Stand up and admit your mistakes (and, importantly, learn from them – always)
- Remain persistent and determined enough to aim for your dream and stick to it, whatever happens or whatever others say.

In terms of skills, no matter what business you start-up and no matter which sector you operate in, there are some skills which are always helpful. These include:
- Creativity
- People skills (because people buy from people)
- Numerical skills (some basic maths is useful, although you can get software to help with doing your accounts)
- Organisational skills.

So let's examine some of these skills in more detail. Take being organised; that's a particularly vital tool for any woman in business. Whether you have children or other caring responsibilities, voluntary obligations, a house to run, or other daily and weekly activities to complete; performing all of these tasks *and* running a business will need incredibly good organisation and planning. You need to be able to juggle and manage your self, your time, your business, your home and your staff.

Being a people person will also make business life much easier. I know business people who don't particularly like people and work for themselves so they can shut themselves off. This is fine up to a point, but, to have a successful business you need customers and you will have to turn on your best charm and pleasantries in order to secure customers and keep them happy. If you expect them to part with their money they will want you to have at least some level of customer service. There are very few business owners who can get away with not caring for their customers. Handling people and their needs well, communicating with them and building relationships based on trust are all key elements to successful business ownership.

Talking about customers leads me on to the importance of selling skills. If, like women I have provided consultancy to, you tell me you don't like selling, you really do need to consider if being a business owner is right for you. Selling is an essential part of any business. If there is no selling, there will be no money coming in, so you have no business, it is actually that simple. You may not find selling as easy as some people; indeed you may hate selling with a passion. However you are going to have to sell and you will improve with practice. To some degree all business owners sell, either direct to customers, to their staff who in turn sell to customers or to third party companies.

If selling is not your thing while it won't be easy, you can learn some basic techniques and there are plenty of books, websites and training courses about selling. I regularly work with women in developing their sales skills and it is possible to turn even the most fearful seller into someone who can sell make sales calls and visits. You can learn to sell.

It's not all about overcoming objections and going for the order. Selling involves treating others as you wish to be treated, knowing what your customers want, listening to your customers, getting the right messages in front of the right people at the right time and providing such fantastic benefit-rich products and services that customers want to share their experience with others. But we'll talk more about how to get your products and services out into the marketplace and make the most of your sales skills later on. For now, let's focus on assessing your skills and abilities:

UTILISING YOUR SKILLS FOR THIS BUSINESS

We have examined the skills you have and you may have started to identify skills you may need to develop. Now you should consider how you can use the skills you have to develop a business. Too often people feel they need to develop new skills to start a business; going on a course on how to be a coach or an aromatherapist . But it is possible to start a business utilising your current skills. If you currently work in a sales department of an estate agent, could you start a business which helps people sell their homes? Or, if you have skills in baking and catering, could you start up a specialist catering firm?

Keep thinking about what you are good at and what skills you have. Look at some other business people and consider what skills they really need. The lady in town that has a clothes shop, what did she do before this? I know two ladies who have successful clothes shops who used to be secondary school teachers. I know a café owner who used to work in IT and a successful photographer who used to work for the NHS and took photos for fun.

Do your skills suit the business you are planning? Are they transferable? Can you apply them to a new business or will you need to learn new skills?

When you are writing your business plan it is worth putting in some background information about your experience and how that can help you in your business. It will help you to also feel more confident about your varied skills and how they will enable you to build this successful business. Consider how varied your experience is and if you have current and up to date qualifications. Now could also be the right time to check if you need any memberships or associations in order to run your selected business. For example, you may be qualified as a physiotherapist, but do you need any specific insurance or membership to a particular body in order to practice professionally?

WHAT PERSONAL CHARACTERISTICS DO YOU NEED?

When it comes to personality traits and characteristics there are some which the majority of successful entrepreneurs share, such as confidence, assertiveness and being sociable.

Being assertive is a skill that I feel all business owners need to have to a degree. You may find it difficult to be assertive. Assertiveness is about being able to express your needs, preferences and feelings in a manner that is neither threatening nor punishing to others. It's about having direct, honest communication between individuals, interacting equally and taking responsibility for yourself. Being assertive is not about always getting your own way. It's not about being arrogant or aggressive. Rather, assertiveness is a balance between self-respect and respect for others, so to be assertive you need to have a sense of your own worth.

When Wendy first approached me to help her, one of her difficulties was her lack of assertiveness. She found it hard to say 'no' to things that she didn't really want to waste her time on. In short she was a 'yes' woman. She also didn't wish to appear pushy with customers when she was selling. Her lack of assertiveness meant her selling skills were weak and her sales message didn't come through clearly. Together we developed her sales technique and helped her to come across more assertive, more confident and more professional. We did this by building Wendy's confidence in relation to her work, her values and her products so that she presented herself and her offerings with confidence and knew what she did and didn't want to get involved in.

Wendy has found this training has helped her to increase her sales and decrease the time spent on unnecessary or time-wasting meetings and projects. She now feels able to say 'no' to requests which don't benefit her or don't help her to achieve her success targets; only saying 'yes' to those which take her closer to her goals.

Confidence

It's easy for me to tell you to be more confident in yourself and your abilities. It's easy to say but less easy to do. However, if you start to focus on and celebrate each of your successes, achievements, skills and experiences, this will help to build your self-confidence and your ability to run your business. Rather than ponder on what you can't do or haven't done; focus on what you can do and have done.

Do you have self limiting beliefs? It is likely that you do as most of us have. Thoughts and beliefs about your lack of ability to carry out a certain task will destroy your confidence and reduce your willingness to try something new. These beliefs have often developed from previous experience and memories. You may have been told by someone else that you can't do something. This negative limiting point starts your brain on a spiral of self doubt and uncertainty in your ability. Constantly being told you are not good enough, can't and shouldn't do something will lead to a lack of confidence and feelings of low self esteem and low self worth.

You need to stop yourself now from carrying on with these self limiting beliefs and start to re-programme your head from an "I can't, shouldn't, wont be able to" attitude to an "I can, should and will be able to" attitude. You may find techniques such as Neuro Linguistic Programming (NLP) or Emotional Freedom Technique can help you, as can working with a coach. It's also useful to realise that there's no such thing as failure as, even if you make a mistake or miss a target, you will learn from that. In fact, it's better to try and fail than not bother trying. You'll learn so much more from the experience if you at least try. That in itself is a great motivator – you can achieve anything you set your mind to and, if you stumble, you'll learn how to do a better job next time round.

A simple tool you can use from today onwards is positive affirmation. There is a link between your conscious mind and your subconscious mind. Therefore, if for some reason your subconscious believes you can't do something then it will tell your conscious mind to believe the same. i.e. If you believe you can achieve something you are likely to make it happen. While if you believe that you can't, it's likely that you won't. What you think often becomes a self-fulfilling prophecy.

A common example is when someone tried to do something and it failed or didn't go as well as hoped. Take, for example, a job interview. If you have previously had bad experiences of going for a job interview, your subconscious tells you this is something you fail at. Therefore, even before you sit down in front of the interviewer, you feel unsure, nervous and may even avoid attending.

It's critical for you to re-programme your brain into believing you *can* be successful in job interviews, by regularly telling your mind, i.e. with positive affirmation, "I am great at interviews and they will want to select me." By regularly telling your brain this next time you need to attend an interview it is far more likely to send these positive messages back to your conscious mind and make your beliefs into your reality. What's more, when you have a more positive interview as a result of this positive thinking, your brain will have been reprogrammed to this more positive experience.

For me confidence comes from really knowing my area of expertise, preparing for situations well and feeling good about myself, the way I look and the way I appear to others. I like to look the part and this helps me in my confidence. However, while I am willing to conform to expectations to some extent (i.e I regularly dress in the suit to conform to the corporate image expected of me) I like to add my own touch like the red shoes I have become so well known for.

WHICH ASPECTS OF THE BUSINESS SHOULD YOU MASTER? OR CAN OTHERS HELP?

Over the years I have worked with both male and female business owners. I have noted that women tend to feel the need to understand everything about their business and are keen to gain the skills that will enable them to carry out all aspects of the business. I am as guilty of this as the next person, spending weeks at evening classes learning simple accountancy. However, I soon learnt that it was a waste of time and money. Doing my accounts is far too painful for me; I absolutely hate it. So I no longer do it. I pay someone else to do it all for me and spend my time on areas of the business that I am good at. My accountant has the expertise and experience to do my accounts well and quickly. The cost amounts to very little, in fact she saves me money, and the time I save in not doing it can be spent on other areas of the business.

Wendy felt to be successful in business she needed to be able to do everything for herself. When she decided to have a web site Wendy spent time and money learning web design. The months of classes and hard work were a bit disappointing and Wendy felt the site she had created didn't really fit the brand she wanted to portray. Wendy ended up paying a web design company to build her a site just six months later. She realised then that she should have just asked them to do it in the first place rather than struggling on with her course when her business really needed her to concentrate on the day to day running of it.

GAINING KNOWLEDGE AND EXPERIENCE FROM OTHERS WILL HELP YOUR BUSINESS

Buying in help, knowledge and experience is perfectly acceptable and, in fact, is likely to help you move your business forward quicker than taking the time to try and learn how to do it yourself. There are some skills which you may need regularly and learning how to do it yourself could be beneficial. Decide realistically what you should learn and what skills you should buy in.

If you can't pay for the services of another professional, try to barter with them. My first website was developed in return for me developing my web designer's marketing plan. I still like to barter now; it's part of the fun of business for me and works well among small business owners.

Ultimately, you can't be an expert in everything. Accept that other people can do things better than you can. Use your time wisely. Using others can give you time to concentrate on the things you are good at.

If you feel you are not ready for business start up yet, maybe you don't have enough experience in the sector you are entering into. If so consider how you could gain this necessary experience. Perhaps you could take a part time or short term job in a firm similar to the one you intend to set up. For example, if you are thinking of opening a restaurant and have never worked in one, you could consider working part time in a restaurant to see if you like it and gain some experience in the process.

Consider as well the skills your family and friends have. Are they willing to help you out, share their expertise or work for you at least in the initial stages? If you need help getting a shop refitted can family members help rather than paying for professional shop fitters? Do any of your fiends have experience of designing logo's or web sites?

During the next stage of the book we shall consider your business idea in more detail. At this point we'll be reviewing your skills again and seeing how helpful they will be to you in your business plans. For now though, it's time to move on to the actual process of business start-up.

REVIEW OF CHAPTER FOUR

- Identify and believe in your personal strengths.

- Consider exactly what you are good at, what you enjoy doing and whether your skills are transferable.

- Don't undermine yourself by dwelling on your weaknesses or failings.

- Think positive. Tell yourself you can and should and will rather than you can't, shouldn't or won't be able to. Be confident and assertive. Believe and you will achieve.

- Don't get hung up on qualifications unless your profession dictates it. Experience, skills attitude and personal qualities are far more relevant to running your own business.

- Review whether you have what it takes.

- Celebrate your strengths and achievements.

- Consider how you can use the skills you have to develop a business.

- Develop new skills appropriate to your business needs.

- Accept you won't know everything and often others can help you. Fill your own skills gap. Seek outside help in areas in which you have no skills and focus your time on areas in which you are skilled at. This may be more cost-effective in terms of time and money.

- Barter services if you can't afford to hire professionals.

STARTING YOUR OWN BUSINESS

IT'S TIME TO PICK UP THE PACE AS WE FLESH OUT
YOUR IDEAS, SET TARGETS AND GET PLANNING

CHAPTER FIVE - DEVELOP YOUR OWN BUSINESS IDEAS

You may already have an idea for your business. However, it could be that all you really know at the moment is that you want to run your own business; but not what, when or how? Whether you have an idea or not, it is crucial at this stage to remember why you want to work for yourself as you focus your mind on developing any ideas that you have. This is the exciting part and you can let your imagination run away with you for a while. You can always review and refine ideas later.

NO IDEA YET?

Finding the right idea for your business may seem daunting. The reality is, most business ideas come from nowhere, quite out of the blue. The best business ideas are simple, useful, and differentiated in some way (so provide something that is better, cheaper, faster or safer than the competition).

- **Consider variations of existing businesses.** Look at other businesses you visit, buy from or know about. Do they offer the complete package? Could you improve on their business idea? Could you offer the same product or service in a different area, marketplace or format?

- **Fill gaps in the market.** Note down any unfulfilled needs. Remember Nicky with her crèche? She started that business because her childcare needs were not being met in her local area. You might decide to start up a gardening service because you can't find someone who will do more than just cut the grass and, when you mention this unmet requirement to others, they all agree and share the same the same problem. Researching the level of demand before you launch your new business is vital. What you and a few friends want may not be a solid enough reason to develop a business.

- **Seek out solutions.** Ask others about their current unmet needs and listen out for the "if only I could get xyz" type of conversations. Most inventions and business ideas are based on someone realising a problem exists which needs a solution. They invent a product or provide a service which provides that solution. For instance, reading by candlelight presented many problems, so much so that Thomas Edison pursued thousands of attempts to invent an alternative solution - the light bulb. That said, be mindful not to pursue a solution to a problem that is non-existent, or you may find that very few people are willing to pay for the solution.

- **Polish your idea spotting antennae.** Keep your eyes wide open. For every product or service you see, consider the business behind it. Take this book, for example, I have come into contact with many businesses during its production: designers, typesetters, proofreaders, book shops, photographers, marketing agencies, PR consultants. I could consider what they offer and how I could offer a better proposition or just do it differently.

- **Record your findings.** Don't narrow your search for a business idea too soon. Many successful business people took months to find their perfect business idea. Keep your eyes and ears open and jot down ideas in your note book; Don't dismiss ideas too easily as even seemingly silly ideas can grow into something bigger and better. Ideas often evolve after going through a process of elimination and can turn into the next big thing.

- **Be Innovative.** Don't be afraid to think differently. When I work with women starting up in business they regularly dismiss ideas as being too different, wacky or off the wall. And yet, the most successful enterprises are generally successful because they are different. These kinds of businesses are called 'disruptive' businesses. They are pioneering enterprises which dare to be different and create entirely new business models that disrupt entire industries. Take Skype, which took on the traditional telecoms industry and provided something completely different to satisfy that industry's large number of unsatisfied customers.

Certainly there is no reason why you can't build a successful business based on an unusual idea. Remember the first mobile phones; and how we mocked them. Few people thought they would take off and there are now more people in the world with mobile phones than with internet connections. Those forward thinking business people who bought into the idea and developed businesses off the back of the mobile phone revolution have been very successful. The first person to charge people to download a silly ring tone, sell a pretty coloured case for phones or charge you to text them a question to answer have all thrived. None of these businesses were around while I was growing up. Which businesses will be around when the next generation reaches adulthood?

- **Focus on what you are truly passionate about.** You need to have passion for your business idea at the beginning because this will help you to keep you going when you have difficult days.

Get yourself a pile of post it notes and a blank wall. Jot down ideas, notes, words and diagrams: one business idea per post it note. Every time you have an idea over the coming days and weeks pop it down and add it to your ever growing sea of post it notes. Regularly review your ideas. Group similar ideas together. Keep adding and removing ideas until you feel you have some really concrete ideas to consider.

BUYING A FRANCHISE

If you can't uncover the right business idea for you to pursue, one option might be to purchase a franchise. Becoming a franchisee gives you the rights (usually paid for by you) to sell a product or run a business developed by another business person using their trademark or business name. The key benefit here is that they generally have proven business models. McDonalds and Coffee Republic are just two well known franchises.

Most franchise businesses work on the basis that the owner of the franchise company charges you to open up one of their shops, agencies, restaurants in your area. They train you and provide you with everything necessary to get the business started. A good franchiser will provide ongoing support and training as well as providing you with new products, marketing materials and ideas to develop your business further. They will usually set out some ground rules in terms of the way in which they will allow you to trade and sell their products. Initial fees are often charged at start up, anything from a few hundred pounds to hundreds of thousands of pounds can exchange hands for a start up franchise. There may also be ongoing fees such as a standard monthly fee or royalties.

BEFORE ENTERING A FRANCHISE AGREEMENT:

- **Do plenty of research.** Look online and in publications such as Dalton's Weekly to find a franchise that suits your area of expertise, your skills and your passion.
- **Speak to existing franchisees.** Find out how they are doing, if they have faced any particular obstacles, what the main challenges have been as well as the main rewards. Don't just take the franchisor's word; ask to speak to a random selection of other people who have set up a franchise with them and also speak to people who run completely different franchises as they may be able to give you pointers and advice to consider.

- **Check the small print.** Consider if there are restrictions on the franchise which makes it difficult for you to grow and develop your business, and check when and how payments must be paid.

Many women like using a franchise in order to start their own business because it provides a relatively low-risk ready-made option. I know many who have then gone on to set up a second business without a franchise agreement, having cut their teeth and learnt about running a business while they were a franchisee. Certainly being a franchisee can be ideal for those new to business. Along with the training and support given you often find they provide most of the materials and equipment required, or, at the very least, have sourced the suppliers for you. This can all take a lot of hassle away.

ALREADY HAVE YOUR OWN BUSINESS IDEA?

If you already have a business idea, it's time to develop it. Investigate your idea and keep developing it until you feel sure it's right for you.

If you are planning on offering a product or service:
- Have you tested it out?
- Have you spoken to others about it?
- Have you researched your market to see if it's something they will buy?

WHY DO YOU THINK THIS IDEA IS A GOOD IDEA?

Research isn't about asking a few friends and colleagues what they think about your business ideas. Frankly they are biased and are likely to say it's a brilliant idea regardless. Also, while pitching to friends can be worthwhile just to see what their response is, this should only be done if they are your targeted audience, if they are really likely to buy from you and represent your planned client base.

GET DIGGING: RESEARCHING YOUR BUSINESS IDEA

Research isn't just about doing a few internet searches and asking some friends and family what they think about your business ideas.

When Joy decided to set up her beauty salon she spent weeks looking into the different products and treatments she could provide in her salon. She started short-listing potential treatments and then looked into what other beauty salons in the area were offering. Some discreet questioning enabled her to identify gaps in the market and possible niche products. Poor Joy also learned that sometimes products are niche for a reason, after having bought a new natural tanning product by the bucket full. Her potential customers had said they liked to look good but preferred if possible more natural products, so it seemed like a great idea; only for her to find that it not only smelt awful, but brushed off onto clients clothes, oops! No wonder no one else was offering it. Joy learned from this mistake and always asks for several samples for her and her staff to try out before committing to anything these days.

Hopefully you will not be making mistakes like Joy, and that's because you are going to take your time to ensure that the products and services you are going to offer are, not only the best you can offer, but are also what your customers will want to buy, at a price they can afford to buy them.

ASK QUESTIONS

Once you have identified your products start asking lots of people lots of questions. Such as: do you buy 'xyz' already? Does it suit all your needs? How could it be improved on? Would you pay more for a better quality product? How often would you buy it? More questions should grow out of the answers you are given.

You can use online free survey tools or walk around the area in which you are planning to sell and ask passers by to fill in your questionnaire. Whichever way you get feedback from your potential clients, listen to it. Many new business owners make the mistake of being so certain their idea will work that even negative feedback from others doesn't put them off or make them review the way in which they will provide the product. Listening to feedback is vital.

Joy also spent time speaking to potential clients when she was out and about, asking about their needs, prices they would be willing to pay and how often they currently use a salon like hers.

EXAMINE THE COMPETITION
Spend time finding out about other similar products on the market. Find out who buys them and, importantly, why they buy them? What reasons do they have for buying alternative products and services? When do they buy, how do they buy and how often? How much do they pay for them? Would they consider buying your product instead? Why so?

Think about it... if you currently use a local hairdresser and a new one opens up do you really think I'll give the new one a try? What would make you try them? Their price, location, parking facilities, loyalty cards? How could they get you to move from your current hairdresser to them? These are the types of questions you need to start considering with regards to your product and potential customers. Big supermarkets moving into a new area will offer good deals and pay for high volume high impact marketing, can you afford to do the same? I doubt it. Consider all of this.

Clare spent time contacting her competition by phone. She asked them about their services, prices and experience. It was not easy for her to do and she was worried that they would know it was her. But it was a valuable exercise for Clare. She was able to evaluate both the competition and their customer care. It helped her tremendously when deciding how she would handle customers.

BE REALISTIC

Have you considered the validity of your research? Lots of potential entrepreneurs on the popular BBC TV programme '*Dragons Den*' fall flat when it comes to the validation of their research. They will have often looked at top line figures and will declare that "the market place is worth £10 million and, if I get 30 % of the market, my business will be worth so many million in year five." Yes, well, if only it were that simple we would all be millionaire business owners. The reality for most people is that they will have a good solid business turning over a reasonable amount of money and making them a good honest salary. A dream is fine but don't base your financial forecasts on pie in the sky dreams and unrealistic research. Back up your assumptions with facts.

When Lucy spoke to her friends and family about starting up in business they were very supportive of her ideas. They all said that her products, services and prices were perfect and she should be really successful. But her friends and family were not likely to be her clients. Their feedback didn't really help her to develop the business in the right way for her customers. The feedback she received from family and friends, whilst well meaning, led Lucy to have a false belief in her business format. It took some time for her to realise that adjustments

97

needed to be made to ensure she was providing her clients with what they needed.

An example of poor product research: We drink 3.9 million cups of coffee in the UK in a week. The global coffee industry is worth £10billion. How much do you think you would take per week in a coffee shop in Cardiff? It's very difficult to tell without considering potential footfall, finding out how much revenue similar establishments turn over in the area, examining how much local competition there is and whether other establishments sell coffee within a certain radius. Yet many business plans show global figures and overall consumption of a product without relating it to their own brand, market place, competition and, crucially to reality.

Consider your existing experience and required industry knowledge. Have you worked in this sector before? Do you know how it works? Do you have a firm grasp with regards to how purchasing is carried out? How marketing is organised? And what the expectations of customers are? I love clothes and shopping for them, but that doesn't qualify me to open a clothes shop. I would need to research the buying of items and the quantities required; how to select suppliers, how to price the items, how to set up the shop in terms of displaying the items and how to handle customers. Much of it I could learn from speaking to others, doing some reading or internet research and I may already have some transferable skills that I could use (such as customer service). However, some good hands on experience would also stand me in good stead for success.

Working part-time in a little boutique may help boost my understanding of the sector rather than relying purely on my Saturday morning shopping trips. However, consider the bigger picture in terms of where you intend to operate once you've gained significant industry know-how.

Don't do as one lady I know did and take a job in a pet shop in a small town in order to learn more about the sector. She wondered why her old boss was less than pleased when she opened a rival pet shop in the same town. An all out war ensued and the more experienced store owner won the day. Experience and industry knowledge will help you get your business from nothing to success with less pain and disaster than someone who has no idea about the sector they are entering. However consider how and where you will gain this industry knowledge.

SELECTING AND MOVING YOUR IDEAS FORWARD

Make a decision. Evaluate and select your idea to move forward. Until you have selected one idea, you cannot get moving forward. There are lots of business ideas out there in peoples heads, on dusty bookshelves and undeveloped. Don't let your business idea be one of them. Map out your ideas, review your research and choose what to focus on. Sometimes you have to go with your gut feeling. What really jumps out at you as a good idea? Which idea do you feel will work best? That is often the right one for you. If you don't feel naturally attracted to a business idea it is likely to be difficult to commit to the business.

If you are still stuck with several business ideas and are unsure which one to commit to, try this activity. Consider your responses to each of the questions below for each of the business ideas you have. Following this review consider how strong each of the ideas now seems.

Your business idea	IDEA 1	IDEA 2	IDEA 3	IDEA 4
Who would you sell your products / services to?				
How clear is your actual business idea?				
What experience do you have of this business or similar businesses?				
Do you know who your competitors would be? What are their strengths and weaknesses?				
How confident do you feel about your idea being a business success?				

HOW TO DEVELOP YOUR BUSINESS IDEA – MAP IT OUT

Now you have your business idea you can mind map it out. If you haven't used mind maps before, now is a great time to start.

Get yourself a big piece of paper (at least A3) and put in the centre a drawing or text box - anything which conveys what your business idea is. The more visual stimuli you place on the mind map the better, as we are trying to ignite the creative side of your brain.

100

Draw some lines off the central section and add suitable sub headings such as; customer needs, competitors, how you will provide the product and the key areas of the business, such as products/services, location, target audience and so on.

Under each heading add your thoughts and research. By mapping it out you can start to see weaker areas which need some more work on before you are ready to move on. You should now have some more detail on your mind map.

If you have more than one idea you can map out each of your ideas. This should help you to move forward in making up your mind about your final business idea.

USE YOUR MIND MAP TO GENERATE ANSWERS

What are the key areas of the business?
- What products/services will it provide?
- Are there any additional revenue streams you could generate and how?
- How clear is your business idea? Could you explain it to someone else in a few short sentences and would they easily understand it? (This is crucial)
- What can you do to clarify your business idea and move it forward?

What will be the driving force of the business? Some businesses are customer led, driven by things that people are already asking for.
- Is the driver the fact you have not been able to source this product locally or even nationally yourself?
- Have you found a need that is not yet fulfilled? Other drivers could be based on things you understand, feel passionate about or have access to.

What are similar businesses offering?
- What's good about the competition and not so good about them?
- What are their strengths and weaknesses?
- Can you see any gaps in their offerings?
- How can you improve on the current business models out there?

What will be your competitive advantage?
- How will you be different from what's already out there?
- What will make your business unique or better than the competition? This could be your level of knowledge or experience.
- Have you been lucky to stumble across a niche market that no one else has tapped into?

DEVELOPING YOUR BUSINESS BRAND

Once you have honed in on one idea, you need to give your business a name. This can be a fun part of starting up your business although some new business owners really struggle with this. It's important to choose a name before you go any further... before you write your business plan, before you set up your website, and so on. **You may have already** come up with some branding ideas while evaluating your values, as discussed earlier in this book.

Branding experts recommend that you should consider something which is simple to remember and relatively easy to understand and say. Some people go for the "Ronseal" approach, using the product they are offering in the title, using the name to clearly reveal exactly what you offer. "Amy's mobile hairdressing" obviously offers hairdressing in a location to suit its customers.

Conversely, business names such as Amazon, Google or Apple don't tell you what their business offers, however, over the years we have associated the name with particular products or services. It doesn't need to mean anything because they have been able to establish their name and brand in such a way that they are household names.

- **Choose a business name which can grow with your business.** Remember, 'Jane's cake shop' is fine when it's just Jane in her shop making cakes, but a few years on when Jane has diversified and is now doing outside catering for corporate events, having 'Jane's cake shop' as the trading name of the business, still on the letterheads and invoices would not be so suitable. Now it looks a bit daft, yet re-branding can be costly and confusing to clients.

- **Check Companies House** (www.companieshouse.gov.uk) and look on the web to see whether your chosen name is a new name or if anyone else has one the same or similar. If this is the case you may not be able to register it – either as a web domain name or as a Limited Company. For example "Amy's Hairdressing" is available but "Amy's Nails" isn't. If you plan to be a sole trader, you don't need to register your trading name with Companies House, but this also means that someone else could register your name and use it as their name.

Take 'Jane's Cake Shop'. As a sole trader, Jane could not stop anyone else in the UK or worse still in the same area opening a shop with the same name. If she was operating as a Limited Company however, she could. Don't fall into the trap of starting as a sole trader with a certain name then finding that you can't register it as a Limited Company once you've built the business up. This can be costly if you have to rebrand and can lead you into trouble if you use a brand name the same or similar to someone else's.

- **Decide whether or not to register your company/brand name as a trade mark.** This is the best way to protect it. To legally register your business name or brand you should speak to a suitably experienced patent, intellectual property or copyright legal advisor. You could also visit www.ipo.gov.uk to learn more about protecting your invention, brand and other important parts of your business known as your intellectual property or IP. Many businesses use the letters TM after the business or brand name to show that they are using it as a trade mark. However, this doesn't make it registered merely it suggests you wish to trademark it.

You should now have identified your business idea; examined it in more detail, considered how you will provide it, come up with a name and possibly looked into suppliers. You are now ready to start thinking about the structure and detail of your business and planning your business. Isn't this exciting? Come on, let's get going.

REVIEW OF CHAPTER FIVE

- Focus on fulfilling unmet needs and providing solutions to real problems.

- Find gaps in existing offerings. Dare to be different.

- Remember simple ideas are often the best. You need to be able to explain your idea clearly in a few sentences. Clarity is crucial.

- Focus on finding a differentiating factor for your business idea. What will make you stand out? What will give you the edge over your competitors?

- Buying a franchise can be a quicker solution to business start-up, but it's vital to research it well as some franchises may not suit your exact needs.

- Consider carefully if the business idea you have really suits you, your areas of interest and the way you wish to work.

- Consider if you have the necessary skills and experience to run this business.

- Spend time mapping out your business idea, as this will be valuable later during the planning process.

- Research, research, research. You can't beat a good bit of solid research to help you develop a strong business idea based on facts rather than dreams. Back up your claims with hard facts.

- Test and validate your findings. Ask questions, gather feedback and listen.

- Choose a name that is simple, easy to remember, understand and say. Make sure it's not already being used.

CHAPTER SIX – YOUR BUSINESS STRUCTURE AND OPERATIONS

HOW WILL YOU RUN YOUR BUSINESS?

Back in the first two chapters we examined why you wanted to run your own business and what your personal needs are. We also looked at what's important to you and how these values and criteria will be reflected in your business. Remind yourself now of these points and then ask yourself the question again: how do I want to run my business? As well as examining the structure of your business in terms of its legal format and what you do, in this Chapter we'll also look at other operational details such as your suppliers and IT requirements.

You may be sure that you want to be running your business on your own. This could be to ensure you have the freedom of being your own boss and are therefore able to take decisions yourself. Others may worry that running a venture on their own could be a lonely journey and decide to move into business ownership with a partner. I know of many women-owned businesses run by two or more women which have been trading successfully for decades. Consider in detail the benefits and disadvantages of working with a partner or working alone – what will best suit you?

Consider your long-term future vision for the business. It is important to know what you want your business to become and where you wish to take it over the course of the next few years in order to decide how you wish to run it from the outset. Think from the start what your long-term aim is.

Take Wendy, for example, her business is run on a part-time basis, a decision she made from the very start. She

106

felt she would be happier in the knowledge that she had a basic salary coming in from an employer to pay her bills, putting less pressure on her to make the business an instant success. She has slowly built up her business but has decided to continue to run it part-time. This works for her and for her personal responsibilities.

Wendy would be the first to admit that, at times, this has been difficult. She could have taken on more work in her business if she didn't work part time as well but, for now, she knows it's right for her. During her business planning stages, she took this into account and set her projections on income and expenditure accordingly. There was no point Wendy spending out lots of money on marketing as it could have brought her more enquiries than she was able to handle. Neither did her plan look at growing with staff, as she knows she wouldn't want that responsibility. Her business plan shows that she will continue in this way for several years. I have a sneaking suspicion the enterprise bug has bitten her however, and that she will start to decrease her hours with her employer to enable her to build up her business, which has been more successful than she thought it would be. Only time will tell.

I see this cautious approach from women regularly. It's a safer and less pressured option, yet they quickly see that the business is growing and then have the option to move into it full time. There is nothing wrong with this approach. I did it myself. However it is hard work juggling everything and you usually get to a point where a decision needs to be made. Doing two things part-time is tough in terms of giving enough attention to either project for them to be the success you wish.

How Will You Operate?

What are you going to be selling and how will you be selling it? Here are a few examples of how businesses operate:

- **Offering a Product** such as a food item, clothing, equipment or baby products
- **Selling a Service** such as a travel agent, catering or gardening
- **Working freelance** such as marketing, journalism or consultancy
- **Earning revenue streams from what you already have** such as renting a house or flat or using your home for bed and breakfast.

Now consider how will you get your product to your customers? Again, there are so many opportunities out there and below are just a few:

- **Online** through your own website, or selling through others such as e-bay or Amazon.
- **Traditional Retail** you could take a shop, part of a shop or a market stall.
- **Direct** door-to-door, via parties in people's homes or at events such as wedding or country fairs.
- **Direct mail via catalogues** sent direct to people, included inside a magazine or in someone else's catalogue.
- **Business to business (B2B)** from an office or your own home.

You need to think carefully about the way in which you will operate and distribute your offerings. It needs to suit you and the product you are offering. If you want to be a florist, selling door to door may not work so well, but you don't necessarily need a shop. You could sell online, from a market stall or through wedding fairs. You may also try to sell direct to a business such as hotels or restaurants. You may even find other resellers who would buy from you, such as garages or corner shops.

LEGAL BUSINESS STATUS

There are three main types of legal status for your business, these are: sole trader, partnership or Limited Company. Your decision regarding the legal status of your business will depend on which best suits your needs and the possible structure and size of your company. There are formal considerations such as tax and VAT, which often depend on the expected turnover and profit of the company. Turnover is the amount of money that comes into the business, whereas profit is the element left from the turnover once all the bills have been paid.

Which legal business structure you decide on will depend on many things including:
- the tax and national insurance you will be liable to pay.
- the type and amount of records you will need to keep.
- the way in which management decisions will be taken.

Each business is unique and, as such, it's best to gain advice from a professional regarding the possible legal status of your company. That said, it's worthwhile knowing the basics, so let's examine your options a little more closely...

SOLE TRADER

The majority of businesses operating in the UK are run by one person as a sole trader. This is a really straightforward way of starting out in business. Registration is simple and record keeping can be kept to a minimum. It is possible to employ other people as a sole trader but, ultimately, you are the person responsible for running and managing the business. As a sole trader the business is not a separate entity, therefore, your personally liable for any debts in the business. In other words, if your business fails, your savings or assets (including your home) could be at risk. Conversely, if you set up as a Limited Company, while obligations and paperwork and tax implications are greater, your personal savings and assets are kept entirely separate.

A sole trader does not register the business at Companies House meaning you avoid the costs associated with that. Nor are you likely to need lawyers or accountants to start your business. You must, however, register yourself as a sole trader with your local tax office before you start trading. You can keep your own records of money in and money out and submit your own tax return. Sole traders often find raising funds for business growth and development more difficult than Limited Companies. You might choose to start as a sole trader and then become a Limited Company later on.

LIMITED COMPANY

A Limited Company is a business registered with Companies House. Its owners (shareholders) have limited liability for the debts of the business up to the value of their shareholding (what you paid for your shares e.g. £1 per share) and they are not personally liable for the company's debts as is the case with Sole Traders. You only need one shareholder for private limited companies and you cannot publicly trade your shares; although shares can be sold to family, employees, other businesses and acquaintances to raise finance for the business. You will be liable to pay corporation tax on profits made in addition to personal (income) tax on your salary, as you will be an employee of the company as well as an employer.

You do have the benefit that a Limited Company is separate to the owner, therefore, if the owner wishes to leave or dies, the business can continue to trade without them. Some suppliers and customers feel safer dealing with a Limited Company. A Limited Company however must trade within a range of legislation which does not always apply to sole traders and partnerships. These can have their own financial and time based burdens. You also need to register the company name with Companies House and submit your annual accounts to them.

To submit your accounts to Companies House you will need an accountant and you may need a solicitor to set up the business in the first place, although there are now many firms who can sell you an off-the-shelf business saving you the time and hassle of instructing a solicitor.

PARTNERSHIP

If, like many other women, you have decided to start up your business with one or more other people, then you could consider setting up as a Partnership. This format means that each partner receives a percentage of the profit of the business. These percentages can be based on investments, time given to the business or other suitable breakdowns. For example, if you form a partnership with a friend who gives £10,000 to help start up the business but only works a few hours a week, you put in the same £10,000 but work full time in the business, you may agree in advance that she is due 35% and you can receive 65% of the profits.

All partners are liable for the debts as is the case with sole traders. If one partner gets the company into debt, all partners are liable. Selecting a business partner can therefore be as big a step as selecting a husband or lifetime partner. Full details of forming a partnership are outlined in the Partnership Act 1890. A Partnership does not register with Companies House and therefore does not need to produce audited accounts, although it should keep adequate accounting records.

You could also consider a Limited Partnership or a Limited Liability Partnership. Both must register with Companies House. However, they have different levels of liability depending on the structure and status of each partner. They are often used by accountants, solicitors, doctors' practices and so on, but can be used by other professions too. Whatever you decide please seek advice and guidance from someone experienced and trustworthy.

OTHER BUSINESS FORMATS

You may also wish to look at setting up a Social Enterprise or a Co-operative. Social Enterprises are businesses often set up as a Limited Company. They trade in the marketplace in order to fulfil specific social aims, often involving bringing people and communities together for some economic development and/or social gain. Social Enterprises often have the aims of tackling social or environmental issues at their core. Profits are ploughed back into the business to further support and enable them in their fundamental aims. More and more business are being established as Social Enterprises.

A Co-operative is an enterprise run collectively and democratically by a group of people, again usually for some specific social aim. There are many hundred co-operatives operating across the country answering many different needs. They usually have wider values and parameters that they trade within than those companies whose prime interest is profit. Being owned and democratically-controlled by their members (members can be individuals or groups and even other enterprises) the decisions taken by co-operatives balance the need for profitability with the needs of their members and the wider interests of the community.

OTHER LEGAL REQUIREMENTS

When it comes to running your business legally there are many requirements. They will vary from business to business but these include some general considerations such as Health and Safety, tax, legal structure, business rates and employment law.

Health and Safety – visit the Health and Safety Executive web site to gain more information about your level of responsibility and requirements. As an employer you have to provide a reasonable level of health and safety for your staff, visitors to

Areas to consider	What would I like my business to look like?	What will I need to consider to enable me to do this?
e.g. hours of business	Open 8am until 6pm in order to meet the need of my customers travelling to and from work	Staff working shifts to cover both ends of the day. Can I realistically be available both ends of the day to supervise opening and closing of shop? Could I maybe take time off in the day to enable me to fulfil other demands?

SUPPLIERS AND DISTRIBUTORS

Finding suppliers who you can trust and rely on will be an essential part of your business start-up phase. Do the research into the suppliers available for your needs, compare them all and speak to others about their experience with suppliers. Don't choose on cost alone, look at delivery: how, when and what will they charge. Find out whether they have minimum order numbers, if they give credit or whether you will need to pay up front. Suppliers will often give deals to new customers, but check the small print, as these can often be linked to bulk purchasing, pre-delivery payment and other options. Remember, the supplier is also in the business of trying to make money and most deals which seem too good to be true often are.

Having said that, it is worth trying to get yourself a good deal. Expect to have to haggle with them a bit. Decide before you speak to suppliers how much you want to buy. Write it down in your note book and try to stick to it. Many new business owners get caught up in the excitement of supplier's catalogues or warehouses. It all looks so good and tempting, but it's vital to have a budget and stick to it. If you think you can sell £40,000 worth of product X in six months then that's how much you want to buy. But do you need it all in month one? Can you afford to buy it all? See if the supplier will send it out in batches. This will help spread the cost and avoid having expensive stock sat in the back store room. Ensure that you don't buy more stock than you can either store or realistically sell.

Remember stock piled up in your store room is money standing still.

Many new businesses find getting credit difficult. Suppliers will often not give credit unless you have a reference from other suppliers to say they have been working with you and you are a safe bet. It may be possible to get a reference from your bank or agree another for of security in order to have products delivered prior to payment. Always enquire about their credit terms; be ready to negotiate but also be ready for them to say they need payment on delivery, particularly as a non-credible start-up.

When Nicky opened the crèche she tried to get some credit agreements and good terms from educational games and toy suppliers but had to resort to using her personal credit card when credit became a problem. Whilst I don't recommend this, many women starting up in business do this. She felt the terms being offered by suppliers were better if she could pay in full before delivery and so furnished and equipped her business using her credit card. Like many entrepreneurs, Nicky took a risk. She was able to pay the credit card off as the numbers attending the nursery grew quickly. It may not have been such a great ending if business had been slower to start with. Nicky could have also tried her bank for support or spoken to a local business support organisation to see if she was able to access support or funding.

When selecting stock and equipment, consider how much revenue or added value they will bring into your business. This will help you decide whether they are too expensive and to get something cheaper or justify their purchase. For example: do you need a till which can do everything but costs thousands when all you need is a basic till which you may be able to pick up second hand?

The amount of money you spend on equipment, stock and other items for your business will affect the prices you will need to charge in order to recoup that money. Set yourself budgets based on realistic expenditure and return on your investment and stick to them. If you're using distributors to get your product into market, keep in mind their margins when pricing your product and the amount it costs to develop it.

Do the maths carefully on all aspects of money coming in and going out of the business. Too often people set up a business based on simplistic research and calculations. For example, if buying product xyz costs me £3.00 which I sell for £5.00 I have made £2.00. But how much did it cost you to sell the product in terms of marketing, storage, delivery costs, staff and all those other incidental things and hidden costs we often forget about. I know you can make money running your own business, but make sure you are being sensible about costs and prices as running a business is one thing but making a profit and a good living from it is totally different.

Spend time creating three versions of your financial assumptions – one pessimistic worst case scenario version, one realistic version and one optimistic version. For example, what if we experience 10% less sales than anticipated and our printer breaks down? It's worth considering all scenarios because, in business, frequently everything takes longer and costs more than we think it will.

TECHNOLOGY REQUIREMENTS

As a small business, particularly if you are operating as a Sole Trader, you won't have your own IT department, so how will you manage when it comes to technology? Take the same approach as you did with other equipment and decide realistically what you will need, from computers and printers to back-up drives, webcams and other add-ons.

The advancement of technology has essentially enabled small businesses to work on a level playing field with larger businesses. It's made the costs of communication, marketing and distribution cheaper. It's enabled us to perform tasks around the clock from anywhere with an Internet connection and sell to a global audience. It enables flexibility and provides easier ways of working. For example you can use wifi for out of office connection to the internet and your e-mails and you might use web cameras, video conferencing tools and internet phones rather than travelling to meetings. Such technology has allowed me and thousands of other women the ability to work more flexibly yet still provide a professional service to clients.

Laptops are also certainly worth considering as they enable more mobility. Many a time have I sat at my son's football training in the car with my laptop. As such I can make best use of any spare time I have: from waiting time in between meetings to time spent travelling on the train. I can also bring it in from the office in the evening once the children are in bed and work on the dining room table, yet I can quickly clear it away when I need to return the house back to a home.

I always recommend investing in a good printer. This will help keep printing costs down as you can often produce professional looking documents on a colour printer without having to pay the high costs of using a professional printer, at least during the initial start up phase. Printing things out yourself and adding a bit of colour on good quality paper can enable you to have a more cost effective and flexible approach to providing printed materials. However make sure they look professional and regularly review using professionals, as there quickly becomes a point were their skills and ability to mass produce at a discount is worth considering.

Remember, doing things yourself is fine but be aware of where your limits are and when you need professional help. Their skills and ability to mass produce at a discount can provide a more cost effective solution.

Whatever you decide with computers and technology, remember the following:
- Keep regular back-ups of your data.
- Arrange for back up support for when technology goes wrong.
- Keep things simple. Make sure you can understand and use the technology you have in place yourself.
- Consider broadband costs and shop around for the deal which suits you and your needs.

- Use an internet café or your local library if you don't use the Internet much.
- Keep e-mails professional. Avoid using generic e-mail addresses, LucyandTim@internetservices.com is fine for your family and friends but not when it comes to maintaining a professional image to clients. Keep the tone and content of e-mails professional and use footers to provide the recipient with your contact details and links to websites.

LIST YOUR REQUIREMENTS

Make a shopping list and ask others if you really will need everything that's on it. Get quotes and check the prices are fair.

When Lucy started her business she told me about the quote she had for professional indemnity insurance. She was pleased she had been given a discount as she had professional membership with an affiliate organisation. However, to me it seemed high and I recommended she get some more quotes. This brief conversation saved her nearly £100 for the same level of cover.

If you're not sure ask someone with experience of business and always shop around.

It may be necessary to accept you will not have as much equipment as you might have benefited from as an employee, at least not to start with. I see many women start in business and try to kit it out in the same way their previous employer did, with expensive computer chairs, desk accessories and shelving. Be realistic. You are unlikely to have your previous employer's budget for equipment and furnishings'. Sometimes you simply have to make do.

It can be fun trying to start up your business on a shoe string; shopping around for bargains and looking for second hand shop fittings, catering equipment and office furniture. When all that money starts rolling in you can always upgrade.

Be clear about what your business will need to operate at a professional level. For example, if your business is office based, do you need the outlay and running costs of a photocopier or could you use a good printer on your computer and make use of the photocopy shop in the high street? Buying everything you need for your new restaurant can be a huge outlay, but is it worth shopping around or looking at second hand equipment?

Remember, all that you spend now needs to be paid back. Many people make the mistake of saying they are happy to invest their savings into the business, but you will one day want to take that initial money back out so it should only be considered a loan to the business from yourself.

Clear planning and thinking ahead about what your business will really need during the start up phase will help to keep you on track. You also need to make sure you don't spend all of your start up money and then realise, once you have started the business that you have forgotten some important items that you can't do without. Think ahead. Don't spend all your money before you even open your doors to paying customers. Keeping a little in reserve will help you out when an emergency happens or you realise you haven't got enough sales in yet and the rent is due. Give yourself a safety net.

When Joy opened her hairdressers and beauty salon she had invested thousands into the salon, buying expensive designer chairs and sinks, leather sofas and amazing mirrors. The salon looked the part and Joy loved it; it was just as she had dreamed it would be. The staff had the very best equipment and products. Joy felt that was important in order to recruit and retain the best staff as well as providing customers with a quality service. Shame then that she didn't buy enough towels and soon found that she couldn't get them washed and dried quickly enough and that the beautiful tiled floor became slippery. Subsequently, in the first few days of trading she had to sort out new flooring and spend on buying more towels, none of which she had planned for, but then she didn't plan for the flood in week six either. Poor Joy didn't have an easy start. Luckily she had the foresight to reserve some money to get her through the difficult times at the start.

REVIEW OF CHAPTER SIX

- Consider your long-term future vision for the business to decide how you wish to run it from the outset. List the pros and cons of different working styles - what will suit you?

- Consider the different types of business status, the implications of tax, management and record-keeping .

- Do some reading before you start planning the business in order to cover all bases, from health and safety to taxation, business rates to employment law.

- Consider whether or not you need a Board of Directors or whether you merely need a mentor or advisor.

- Research and compare suppliers examining cost, delivery, minimum order requirements, credit deals and so on.

- Consider how much revenue or added-value stock and equipment will bring into your business. Justify each purchase.

- Devote time to figuring out all incomings and outgoings. Work out pessimistic, realistic and optimistic versions of the figures. Consider hidden costs. The devil is in the detail.

- Harness the power of technology to save time and money and truly enable your business yet only spend on technologies that you really need.

- Understand your limits in terms of skills, time and equipment and when to outsource tasks to others.

- Shop around for bargains. Have a safety net in terms of some money in reserve for emergencies.

CHAPTER SEVEN – WHAT WILL SUCCESS LOOK LIKE FOR YOU?

Before tackling the planning process, it's important to consider what success will look like for you and set appropriate targets to strive towards. But what is success? Success to my ten year old son was being able to play Away in the Manger on his guitar in the school Christmas play. Others listening to him would say that's not success because it isn't perfect. But is success about achieving perfection or achieving a personal goal? As parents and teachers supporting him we have been keen to tell him how well he is doing as this is boosting his confidence and encouraging him to keep going and improve over time. Being told you are not a success does nothing for your confidence.

I want to share with you now one of my key principles to being a success in business. That is to set and believe in your own success targets. Please don't set yourself up in business based on other people's success targets. I have met too many women over the years who believe they are not a success. When asked why, they often tell me because they are not as good as ...so and so, who they perceive as successful.

Let's get one thing straight right now; you are setting up your business for *you* and not for anyone else. There is too much of a culture of comparison in this country, rather than celebration of individual successes based on individual targets and perceptions of success. Therefore it is up to you to measure your level of success. I feel strongly that having some targets to aim for is a great driver when you work for yourself. These success targets can be reviewed and tweaked as you and your business grow. They should also be multi levelled; a year from now, five years from now and even more long-term. So before planning begins, consider your success targets based on your own vision of success – what do you wish to achieve and why?

YOUR PERSONAL SUCCESS TARGETS

While you should think big and reach for the sky, it's important to get a good balance between realism and ambition to avoid setting unachievable targets. There's no point dreaming of running a business which allows you to work five hours a week for a typical football player salary; that would be based on fantasy not reality. Goals should be SMART (Specific, Measurable, Achievable, Relevant and Time Bound).

"The greatest danger for most of us is not that our aim is too high, and that we might miss it, but that it is too low and we reach it". – Michelangelo

Being in business is a non limiting experience. Unlike working for someone else, when you run your own business, you have control and can move it in any direction you want at the pace you want. You can use your move into entrepreneurship to give you the life you desire, to pursue a career you've always dreamed of, as a platform to gain experience and gain a high profile position or get involved in local or national politics. Only you can decide what you wish to achieve and work towards it. In doing so you should aim for the right balance to achieve a manageable level of success: too low and you have nothing to aim for; too high and they will seem unachievable and unrealistic. The world is your oyster and together you and I are going to get you moving towards your dreams.

Over the years I have witnessed that setting realistic and achievable SMART success targets is a worthwhile motivator and driver for women in business. Focusing on specific targets and having the determination to achieve them means that these women generally do so. Obviously it's no good setting unachievable and unrealistic success targets or I would have a business which sees me unable to work

The level of success strived for by many business owners I know is for the business to earn enough for them to have a good standard of living while still having time for themselves. This makes the business manageable and thus enjoyable for them. You too may be happy to have a smaller 'lifestyle' business but a better way of life – for you, that may be what success is all about – achieving a healthy work-life balance through working for yourself. Conversely, you may strive for a higher level of success and wish to sacrifice work-life balance initially to build a high growth company and sell it on for a large sum via a strategic exit. You might choose to expand rapidly by creating a franchise model or expanding with more staff, more shops, more offices...

My clients fit both of these ends of the perception of success scale. They vary from those whose success targets are to earn enough to buy a mini to those who wish to buy a Ferrari; from women for whom success equates to having their own art exhibition to others who feel success will be reached when they sell their business for over a million pounds. Whether you wish to be comfortable or wish to become a millionaire, the right level of success is determined by what success looks like to you personally.

Use the table below to start considering your individual success targets a year from now, five years on and into the future.

Example's	Year from now	Five years from now	The future
	Start business up Open first shop	Can afford my own home Have 4 shops and online sales	Can afford to work less Have sold the business for £
Success Target 1			
Success Target 2			
Success Target 3			

Think now about what success is to you and how it will look for you when you have achieved success. The targets above, how you achieve them (more on that in the next chapter) and your vision of success will be your Critical Success Factors (CSFs) which will keep you motivated whilst establishing and running your business. They will also help you to avoid doubts about yourself and your success by having clarity so you are clear when you have achieved your targets and are therefore successful. Consequently you will no longer need to measure success based on other peoples' success targets.

FUTURE LONG-TERM SUCCESS
As your business progresses it will be valuable to revisit your success targets. I recommend you do this as a minimum on an annual basis, preferably quarterly. Also, don't forget that many of us change as life changes or as we grow older. Things which were once important may hold less importance while things that never used to be important, suddenly become so.

You may find that, as you and your outlook on life change, so does the focus of your success targets. For instance, when I was younger my business success targets were based on increasing staff numbers, growing profits and client numbers. However, now they are more about my personal level of achievement and my work life balance.

I suggest you buy a small notebook and write your success targets for this year on the first page. Review these targets regularly over the next 12 months. Tick off any that you have achieved. Then, next year, write your success targets out fresh on the next page. Some of the longer term ones may be repeated; that's fine. Repeat this process year on year. Review previous targets occasionally but, on the whole, keep moving forward, altering your success targets as you need to and ticking off those that you achieve. Using this simple technique will enable you to stay focused on what is important to you and not to others.

Clare regularly struggled with confidence during her early years in business, even as she began to achieve more and more in her business and personal life. She often spoke to me about not being a success. We discussed what success looked like to Clare and what she would feel like when she was successful. It soon became obvious that Clare felt she was not as successful as other people seemed to be.

What was happening to Clare regularly happens with the women I meet. They are running their lives and business based on other people's ideas of success. (Also other people may appear to be more successful than they actually are; they may have the trappings of wealth but be up to their necks in debt). Comparing success levels is futile.

ACHIEVING YOUR SUCCESS TARGETS
The first and most important part of achieving is BELIEVING. As such it's vital to avoid negativity.

We touched on the impact of belief in Chapter Three on values and we will talk about this some more. The point is that being positive about yourself and your business will drive you towards achieving your personal success targets. It is therefore crucial to avoid people who push their negativity onto you. Only share your success targets with people you trust who will be positive with you and supportive of your plans. I rarely share my success targets with others as they are my personal desires and I don't wish others to impose their self-limiting beliefs on me.

Of course, as a human being, you will most probably have your own self-limiting beliefs; those nagging feelings and thoughts which stop you from doing things. You may think: "Who am I to want this?" or "I don't deserve this." Additionally you may feel "I can't do this" or "I won't be able to do this." Promise yourself from now on that you will avoid these self-limiting thoughts. Whenever you feel any of them entering your mind, think about something else. Instead you need to concentrate on what you *can* do and how you *will* achieve. By doing this and concentrating on your success targets you will achieve what you set out to. What's more, you will be able to achieve something you can feel proud of.

The second part of achieving is having a clear plan of action: a route map outlining how you'll reach your destination.

Once you know WHAT you wish to achieve, you then need to figure out exactly HOW you will achieve your objectives. For example, if your long-term goal is to sell the business for large sums of money, you need to set up your business in such a way that it will be attractive to someone else to buy it.

Nicky knew from day one that she would have to work very hard in her business to make it a success. However being a good mum and spending time with her children was also important to Nicky. So in order to achieve both success as a mum and a business owner she had to accept some compromise. Building the business into the smooth running highly reputable business she wanted took a little while longer than if she had thrown herself into it day and night. In order to keep things running smoothly even when she wasn't there Nicky recruited in a highly experienced nursery manager. This did mean Nicky couldn't earn as much as she wanted to initially but it did enable her to build a quality business quickly whilst not compromising on her time with her own children.

Nicky actually believed this made her both a better mum and business owner. She knew both needed her time and energy but each were important and needed to be considered when making decisions in her life.

As successful entrepreneurs will tell you, you need to have the end in mind and even have an idea of who might acquire your company from you from day one. You need to list potential suitors, find out what their own long-term strategies are and build your business to suit their requirements as well as your own. Ultimately, if your aim is to develop a business which you can sell for big bucks, seek advice from others with experience in this during the start up stage of your business. If, on the other hand, you wish to run a business that pays you a good enough salary to be comfortable and secure rather than hugely wealthy, consider how you will achieve that goal. What do you need to do in order to make that happen? Always start with the end in mind and flesh out your plan of action from there.

So, about that planning process... it's now time to consider HOW you'll achieve the level of success you desire and reach your targets.

REVIEW OF CHAPTER SEVEN

- Imagine now what your success will look like for you. Have a picture in your mind; visualise achieving your level of success. Start with the end in mind.

- "Believe and you will achieve." Avoid listening to negative people who can't understand your desire to be a success or who scoff at your own personal success targets. Set and believe in your own goals.

- Ensure your goals are SMART (Specific, Measurable, Achievable, Relevant and Time Bound).

- Review your own individual personal success targets regularly. Don't limit yourself or your levels of success to those you currently have, as these may change and develop over the years. You should therefore review and develop your success targets periodically.

- Accept your success and celebrate it. Pat yourself on the back when you achieve your targets. You deserve it!

CHAPTER EIGHT - YOUR BUSINESS PLAN

How much planning goes into your annual holiday? What effort did you last put into planning when you last moved house? How about planning of Christmas, family excursions and relationships? Yet many people spend very little time planning their business. They get so excited about their idea, or so anxious that they need to hurry and get their product/service out there into the marketplace before anyone else, that they rush and keep planning to a minimum. And yet this is a business which, in all honesty, could change your life, hopefully for the better. As such, if you are serious about this business, you need to start planning right now and give it the time and attention to detail that it deserves.

It's all too common for me to see people starting a business without really taking the time to consider the business plan, how this business will actually work and who will be their customers. It's a sure fire way towards business failure to be honest. Very few people can get away without some initial planning and still have a successful business. This time spent planning now is time well invested.

So, let's start to fill in some of the blanks for your business plan together. I can't tell you everything about business planning in one chapter, but this should give you a really strong starting point, and give you pointers as to where you can gain help and support in writing a business plan.

Remember this business plan is for you, but you can also use it to gain support from others as well. You might use it to persuade financiers to finance your business, to generate interest from potential partners or simply to help ensure that you make informed choices about each aspect of your business, create a winning strategy and stick to your route. Whoever the audience of the plan is for, this chapter is about ensuring your business gets the best start it possibly can.

Writing your business plan should be an exciting aspect of your business start up. This is where your dreams are beginning to turn into reality.

TOP TIPS

- Keep a notebook in which to sketch out your business plan. You can jot down all the little ideas you have, however silly they seem; recording all the things you need to know or need to do; all the ideas and the inspirations you have.
- Use your business plan to express your ideas and vision for your business; no one says the plan has to be all text and figures. You can add pictures, images and drawings which help to explain how your business will look and feel.

WHAT IS A BUSINESS PLAN?

A business plan is not only a document which explains what your business is and what it will do. Essentially it is a bit like a map which outlines your destination (your success targets and overall vision for the business) with details about what you need to do on the way to make it happen and reach that destination. It therefore also covers how your business will be run, who your customers will be and where they will come from.

Financial, management and legal information about your business should also be included. All of this data works to provide a case for why this business is viable, why your destination is reachable.

You may feel you don't need a formal written business plan, particularly if you are not seeking outside financial help, and this may be true to a certain extent. But, it is a mistake to think you can do without it completely. It's so much easier to reach your destination if you know where you are going and how to get there. At the very least you need a simple document which outlines your business, its focus and where you anticipate it going. Certainly, if you need to access business support, grants or loans, or if you need to deal with a bank for a business account, loan or overdraft facility, they will all expect to see your business plan.

Your business plan will hold all the information about your business, where it is going and how it will get there. This will help keep you focused on your future and the success you are aiming for. When writing the plan refer back to the elements we have already discussed about what you wish to achieve, how you wish to work and so on, to make sure you are keeping on track in developing a business you really want to run. Keep in mind at all times what is important to you.

WHY WRITE A BUSINESS PLAN?

1. Noting things down will free up your mind, keeping it clearer for creative thinking and less cluttered with all the minutiae as they are now being recorded for later referral.
2. It gives you focus. Ultimately, writing things down in a sensible format is well worth the effort as it will help you focus your ideas to give them clarity and will keep you on track.
3. It gives you direction. It enables you to consider your long-term vision and set your targets en route to help you reach your desired destination.
4. It ensures you collect all the necessary information before you jump headlong into starting your business and gives you the chance to identify and tweak weak

areas, check the viability of your ideas and make informed strategic decisions going forward.

5. It provides you with a tool for securing finance. Banks, anyone you approach for a grant or loan, investors, landlords and even some suppliers and large customers will want to see your plan. They need reassurance you have thought this idea through and understand the implications of running your own business and how it will work. They need to minimise their risk of investing in you (or supplying/working with you). By examining your financial planning and getting reassurance that you understand the need for cash flow (that is that money is coming in faster than it is going out) and how you will keep the business afloat during the early stages, they are more likely to give you what you want, be it money, stock or custom.

Essentially, anyone looking at a business plan wants to get a feel for how likely this business is to succeed. They need to understand what it will be offering, (believe me, I have read many business plans and got to the end without knowing what the product is) how it will provide it and who will be buying it. They also want to know how the business will be managed, by whom and what experience you have. They will also look at what research and evidence is supporting the business idea to justify any assumptions you make. So, let's look at what you should include in order to paint a clear picture of your business vision and reassure yourself and any other stakeholders that you and your business are worth working with and believing in.

THE BUSINESS PLAN STRUCTURE
Your Business Plan should consider the period prior to start up, the first year of trading and at least some suggestions of the way forward for the business over the next two years, taking you up to year three.

You can decide how long and how detailed your business plan is; there is no right or wrong length. Equally, there is no perfect list of what should be included within a business plan. However, I suggest that you use the areas I have mapped out below to get started. You can always add other things which you feel are important to your business later on. There are lots of free business plan templates on the Internet or available from business support agencies. Alternatively you can get more information about business plans from banks and books.

Ideally, try to include the following content in your business plan (I will explain some of these in more detail below):
- Your business name, your name, address and contact information, plus business status details
- List of contents
- An executive summary outlining where you are now and where you want to be
- The business idea. i.e Your products/services and Unique Selling Point (USP) details
- Your marketplace (customers and competition)
- Operations and facilities
- The management team and personnel
- Your marketing and sales plan
- Financial data
- Appendix (including CVs of key personnel, elaboration of statistical data, etc).

THE EXECUTIVE SUMMARY

Start your plan with an Executive Summary. This will act as a taster to the rest of the plan. Some people may only read this part of your plan and make up their minds based on this section whether it is worth reading the rest, so make this clear, readable and simple to understand. Also keep it positive and make sure the reader will understand exactly what your business is all about once they have read it. Put in the key points of your plan and outline what your plan is trying to achieve, i.e. help raise funds, map out your business, and so on. Summarise where you are now and where you want to be in the future. Crystalise your vision here.

You may find it easier to write the Executive Summary last. For now though, I suggest you pop down the four main aspects of your business you feel people need to know about. They will vary in complexity depending on the nature of your business. For example: I will be running this business as a sole trader offering mobile chiropody to customers in their own home. My customers will fit into two main groups (professional time-starved people and elderly retired people) who will benefit from my key Unique Selling Points which will be xyz. I intend to trade from the 1st of April this year and will work a minimum of 30 hours a week. In setting up the business I will require some equipment priced at £xxx to enable me to xyz. You get the idea; why not make a start below?

The four main aspects of my business are:
1.
2.
3.
4.

THE BUSINESS IDEA

This is where you can at last put in some information about your business proposition: i.e. the services or products that your business will provide. Start with a brief description of the business. The length of this description will depend on whether this is a variation on a traditional business, in which case it won't need to be very lengthy at all, or whether the business is unique, in which case more explanation may be required. Either way, clarity is vital here.

Make sure your 'Business Idea' section is flexible being careful not to rule things out at this stage. For example,

138

when Nicky began planning her crèche, she didn't anticipate the need for an after school club in her area, so said in her business plan that she wouldn't be offering care for school aged children. However, only months into opening her doors, she had so many enquiries that she started looking into after school and holiday care.

She then had to go back and amend her plan and re-submit it to the bank, as she needed even more financial support from them. It wasn't a big problem but it did cause more work for her during a very busy time. It would have been better to have considered this possibility by researching whether an after-school club might be required before starting up. That way she could have sought the additional finance from the outset. That said, change is constant in the world of business and bank managers generally are aware of this. Flexibility is crucial.

If you are going to have lots of products, you may not wish to list them all, but it is wise to group the type of products/services you will offer.

Your Marketplace
Understanding your market is one of the most vital considerations. Have you identified who your market is? Who do you anticipate will be buying from you?

- Summarise here who your potential customers are going to be. Create a customer profile. Who are they? Where are they? How will you find them? How will they find you?

- Explain who your competition is and how you will differ from them. Why will your customers choose you over what's already out there?

For example, if you are planning on selling wedding cakes, your market might include mothers of the bride, the bride to be, wedding planners and venues who arrange weddings. Once you have identified your target market you should consider how far you will be willing to travel to deliver the cakes: 10 miles, 50 miles, 100 miles? You can then establish how big this market is. There may be data about how many weddings are held on average in your area each year. You would then be able to say you are aiming for 10% or 20% of the market in the area. You should also note down who else offers wedding cakes within that radius and what makes you better than them.

Being realistic about how big your market is and checking that your products match the needs of your possible market is of crucial importance. Too many businesses either pretend the market is there or never investigate it in advance. They then find themselves in business battling to get sales because, they either don't know who their audience is, or their market simply doesn't want their product.

Ask yourself the following questions and write down the answers in your business plan.

- Is the market you have identified large enough to cover your costs and bring you in an acceptable income stream plus provide you with opportunities for growth?
- Is your potential share of the market you have identified realistic for you to achieve?
- What is the level of demand for your product within your identified market?
- Do you have a firm understanding of the specific needs of your target market?
- Is the market likely to grow in the coming years, remain static or decline as many businesses have recently experienced? Why so?

Take this book for example, the market is certainly growing for products aimed at budding entrepreneurs because more people are starting their own businesses than ever before. While the book is specifically aimed at women, my target market is not all women, as the reality is that not all women would buy a book about starting up a business. The most entrepreneurial age for women in the UK is, according to research, 35 – 44. So I have now narrowed down my main demographic target market to women aged 35 – 44. I could then dig deeper to find research on the type of women who are more likely to run a business: what professions are they currently in? Which parts of the country do they live in? What publications do they tend to read? And so on.

Your demographic market could be families with young children or retired couples with a reasonable income. Once you've worked out who your main demographic market is, research the number of people who fit into this demographic within your anticipated business trading area. For example, if you are planning on setting up a family restaurant aimed at young families with children under 12, you may already know that people don't travel more than 15 – 20 miles to visit a restaurant. This means you can find out how many families who fit your requirements live within that radius of your proposed restaurant. You might then survey a small proportion of those families to see what percentage of your selected families eat out, could be persuaded to eat out and when they do so. You could then say 10% of the x number of families in this area eat out or could be persuaded to eat out – that's your target market.

The example I have given you above is a very basic market segmentation. By knowing your market it will be easier to find out how they buy, what their needs are so you can tweak your proposition accordingly, and how to get your messages in front of them. For example, with this book, if I know my main market will be women aged 35-44, then I need to find which publications they read to put an advert in. I might also try to get some free marketing through an interview with that publication or maybe an interview on a radio programme that women of that age group listen to. I might also discover that this age group of women tend to buy their books from online retailers in which case I'd focus a lot of my marketing on online discussion groups and book review sites and ensure my publishers got the book distributed on sites such as Amazon.co.uk.

Similarly, if I wish to sell prams to expectant mothers, I would try to find out whether they are happy to buy from a website or catalogue or whether they prefer to see it in a shop and try the pram out. Including details about how people buy in your business plan along with how they find the products they need is vital. Do they research it in a magazine or on the internet? Do they ask other expectant mothers or mothers with babies? Do they follow trends or those celebrities use? All of this data about your market should be included in the marketing part of your plan. We have already covered the importance of researching your target market and assessing what's already out there in terms of the competition in Chapter Five.

In your business plan you need to spell out what your competitive advantage will be. What gives you the edge over your competitors? You need to essentially make sure your products will be better than your competitors. In order to do this you need to know:
- what your target market wants/needs
- what your competitors do and don't offer.

Research local and/or national gaps in the market. Taking an idea that works in one area and moving it to your own area could work. But make sure people in your area have the same needs and desires as those in the area where the idea originated. For example, a dog walking service may work well in a city environment with time-starved professionals wishing to have their pet cared for. But move that service to a countryside location and you may find that potential customers don't need or want to pay for such a service, or they will be so spread out so you wouldn't be able to take on as many clients per day.

Conversely, you may find that people are just as time-starved in that location and that more people have dogs than in the city location. The point is, you need to find out. Do your homework when it comes to your marketplace, its needs, size and potential for growth.

| **List down who you believe to be your target market.** |
| E.g. parents, business owners, teenagers. |
| |

| **Now be a bit more specific about your target market.** |
| E.g. parents with children under the age of 6 months |
| |

| **How will you find your target market?** |
| E.g. adverts in parenting magazines, online parenting forums, social networks, antenatal groups, local noticeboards, and so on. |
| |

| **How does this target market currently buy similar products?** |
| E.g. online, reading about them in magazines, via word of mouth, impulse buying, following trends |
| |

Carry out plenty of research about your intended market and their buying power (how much can they spend and how frequently?) How often would they need to buy? Who do they currently buy from? How happy are they with the current supplier and would they consider using a new supplier? You can carry out surveys online, face-to-face or over the phone; hold focus groups and speak to potential clients.

HOLD A FOCUS GROUP

Focus groups can be easily arranged by asking different types of people who all fit into your demographic target sectors to come along for a free coffee or glass of wine so that you can talk to them about your new business idea. Tell them in exchange for a drink and some free samples you would like their feedback and help. Make it fun and include them in decision making about product names, packaging, logo design, and so on. Try to choose people who suit your intended market segment (although it is worth trying to get varied feedback across multiple fields from different parts of your overall target market in order to build a bigger and more realistic picture) and ask them if they can bring along a friend who also suits your business customer profile. As well as providing you with some useful feedback, this exercise could even bring you your first customers.

OPERATIONS AND FACILITIES

This section of your business plan takes into account the operations side of business. How will the business be run? Who will supply you? How will you distribute your wares? What assets will you have and where will the business be run from in terms of premises? List here the computers and other technology that you will be using along with any procedures relating to customer service, communication and distribution. Also list anyone involved in your supply chain.

Outline the cost of buying, renting or leasing equipment and premises and anything else that you realistically need to run your business. When I started my business there was only me and one computer, but once we started to grow I needed staff and they needed computers. However, it wasn't that simple, as we soon needed to link those computers together and needed a server. That was something I hadn't planned for in the size of office I rented, nor did I have the finances in place to enable me to arrange this immediately.

Whilst easily solved by an IT expert we bought into the business, using our own computers to link up, it became a distraction for a while, keeping me away from the important aspects of running and growing the business. It is therefore far better to plan for potential big expenditures like this. If you know that you are likely to grow your team from just you to four people and will need to buy a server in order to offer networked functionality, state when you think this might happen and how you will afford this change.

THE MANAGEMENT TEAM AND PERSONNEL

It's a good idea to include some background information about you here, including details of your experiences, skills and knowledge. Refer back to Chapter Four where you have already identified these. In this section you don't need to include your CV (I would suggest only including your CV and those of key personnel in the Appendix section at the end, and only if it is relevant. A CV which shows you have no experience or knowledge of the business you are entering may do more harm than good). Here you only need to include an overview and a personal profile which highlights why you can run this business. If you have identified areas where you are lacking the skills or experience required for your business, you can identify how you will fill this gap either through learning and developing those areas yourself or by recruiting someone with the necessary skills and experience required.

You will need to put in some detail here about the proposed structure of your business. If you already have people in place, pop a little staff chart in here showing the levels of authority. Any staff still required can be shown as empty posts. If this is the case, I recommend you add in the likely dates when you feel you will need to have this individual on board and why you'll need them. You will also need to show this in your financial plans so it can reveal how the business will pay for different staff members and when they can be brought on board.

For every member of the management team or people on board with specific skills, include a few lines about their experience, qualifications and what they bring to the business. Also note down any companies or employees who will be particularly key to your business. For example, if you will be a web based business and you have no web authoring skills you may have already recruited a web designer and will need to demonstrate that in your plan.

An investor may ask how you will ensure this person doesn't up and leave you without the ability to run your business. Your answer might be that you have offered them shares in the business or an incentive package, or you might have a back up plan in case you need to replace them. Whatever your plans are involving key people, explain them clearly so anyone reading your plan can see how this business will be managed and run, not only on day one, but into the future too.

This would also be a good time to identify how you will recruit, train, retain and pay staff. How you will motivate your team? Also consider what gaps you may have in your team at various times of trading, such as during the start up phase, and how you will manage that, whether that will be by learning to do the task yourself, bringing in a freelancer or a hiring a temporary member of staff.

Your Marketing and Sales Plan

1.	**Outline exactly how your marketing will increase your opportunity for sales.** Set yourself a marketing budget and show how you anticipate spending it. Money spent on a good marketing campaign can quickly add up. You need to consider what return (income from customers generated as a result of your marketing activities) is required to make expenditure worthwhile. What marketing tools will you use to get your messages in front of the right people at the right time? Will you use adverts, direct mail campaigns, take a stand at an exhibition or set up a web page? In short, what will your marketing and sales strategy be and why?

2.	**Set targets for anticipated sales.** Identify the average price of your products or services and realistic sales. These will give you some idea of the anticipated income levels. Don't get excited yet, this is turnover rather than profit, but more about figures below. For now, just concentrate on identifying realistic sales potentials. If you have already tried selling your product you may be able to use this as a basis for identifying future sales.

Be realistic! I once visited a lady in a clothes shop who had anticipated minimum sales of £2,000 a week. Yet, with the average price of a garment in her shop being only £40, she would need to sell 50 items a week. When I pointed that fact out to her she gasped that she was lucky to have 50 people come in through the door each week in her rural shop, let alone for each of them to buy something. Whilst her target may not have seemed that much to her at the beginning it was hardly realistic given the garments she was selling and the location of the shop. With all her financial forecasts based on these new anticipated sales figures her business seemed less healthy than her previous business plan, but at least it was realistic and meant that she would only spend on the amount of stock or equipment that she really needed.

147

When I set up my Women's Network I spoke to other networks about the number of people that they usually had attending events. I uncovered how much people were willing to pay and what they expected for their money. I was also able to speak to other women's networks and get their advice on expected sales and costs. This all helped me in writing my business plan and setting some realistic sales targets early on. I was able to do this as no one saw the network as a threat to them so they happily shared their experiences with me.

You may not be able to ask direct questions as I could, however you could try some indirect questions. For example, the hairdresser in town will let you know if her salon is busy and asking to make an appointment will show you how easy or difficult it is to get an appointment. Furthermore, other local people may be able to tell you if they have to travel far to a specialist hairdresser or struggle to get an appointment or find parking or get a good level of customer services. All of this will help to build up a picture of the marketplace for your hairdressers. This type of research is not enough on its own but it is a starting point for you.

Financial Data
Things get a lot more serious here and I would advise you to get some help if you don't know much about financial planning for a business, either from the many websites and books out there, or you may qualify for some free advice from government funded enterprise agencies.

Financial details are vital parts to support your business plans and justify whether your business will work. In business you need to make money in order to survive and, not only make money, but make more than you spend in order to make a profit rather than incur a loss. That said, many businesses incur a loss in the first year or so of trading as they grow their business and gain momentum.

How Much?

The first element to consider is the start-up capital you require. i.e. how much money you realistically need to get started, both to buy the necessary equipment (capital investment) and to pay for things such as rent, insurance, salaries and so on, right from the beginning.

Start to identify the necessary investment or funding you will need and how you plan to gain this. If it's from several different sources explain what these sources and types of finance are (for example, you may use a blend of savings, bank overdraft and loan facility, new business grant and equity funding). Once the source(s) has been confirmed, add this into your plan. For example, if you have already confirmed a loan from the bank of 40% of the start up costs and you have another 20% saved, show this in your plan so that a person reading it can see you still need 40% but you have made the effort to secure the rest. It also shows that others, including you, are willing to risk investing into the business. Banks and investors are unlikely to invest if you are not putting your hand in your own pocket, unless you have a truly mind-blowing idea.

Typical sources of finance include:
- grants
- your own savings
- family and friends
- bank loans and overdrafts
- credit cards
- business angel and other equity investors.

Once you have totalled up your start-up costs, the second element to consider is how much you will need for initial running costs, such as paying bills, buying stock, paying the rent, paying wages of staff and not forgetting your own living expenses and any costs relating to financing the original start up costs, such as loan or credit card repayments..

You will also need to demonstrate when you will likely be able to pay the investors back and, in the case of equity investors, what kind of return they will see on their investment. Consider also what would happen if someone demanded payment sooner. Could you manage to re-finance or raise the money elsewhere?

It is important you feel happy about the financial side of things from the beginning. You must know your financial planning will hold water. However, all too often I see people become disheartened at this stage. They start to worry that their business will never happen and put it on the back burner. The reality is you have to take a leap at some point.

CASH FLOW AND PROFIT
To be a success your business needs to make profit. But to stay in business and keep trading you need cash or cash flow. Many businesses fail, not because they are not a good idea or potentially profitable, but because they have run out of cash. They might have lots of big clients but, because the money is going out faster than they can keep it coming in, they run out of cash and sink. Remember, in business cash is king. Many good businesses fail because they don't have the cash in the bank to keep their business running.

With that in mind I can't tell you enough how important it is to keep up to date records. Doing so will help you keep an eye on the cash flow, be aware of possible shortfalls in the business and keep you running legally, smoothly and professionally. Get yourself a simple system in place for handling all paperwork, especially legal and financial aspects. If this is an area you find yourself struggling in, consider buying in help for this aspect of your business. It will be money well spent.

When Clare took over the business she was determined to do everything herself, keeping the legal paperwork

150

and documentation and accounting side of the business going whilst being involved in the business on a day to day basis. However, the reality of the situation meant Clare would often find herself throwing bits of paper at her desk while trying to juggle telephone calls, dealing with staffing issues and handling stock deliveries. This resulted in a confusing non-existent system.

Subsequently, when Clare came to complete her VAT or Tax returns, or do her payroll documentation, she spent much of her time hunting for relevant pieces of paper and re-entering data which had been entered incorrectly.

I asked Clare to calculate how long she spent each month on financial matters and then consider how comfortable she felt doing this aspect of the work. It transpired that she spent at least ten hours per week on invoicing, payroll and so on. What's more, she really didn't like doing it and didn't trust herself that she was doing it the best way for her business or correctly. Clare decided then to hire a professional to work for her for one day a week. They completed all the work which previously took Clare ten hours and to a much higher level, often helping Clare to save money. The ten hours saved meant Clare could concentrate on other areas of her business, such as generating more sales. What's more, Clare now had peace of mind that the job was being done properly. Clare knows the one day she pays for is excellent value for money and relieves her from the stress of work she feels ill prepared to do.

Consider the true cost of running your business and look at the figures for running the business for a minimum of a year but preferably three years. Doing all of this will help you cost out your products, decide if the initial investment can be realistically paid back, and ultimately recognise whether the business will be able to pay you a realistic salary that is worth your time and effort.

SWOT: A TOOL TO HELP YOU WRITE YOUR BUSINESS PLAN
Use a SWOT to help you develop your ideas and plan. A SWOT examines the Strengths, Weaknesses, Opportunities and Threats of the business. Essentially, these are the areas that you will need to consider while you develop your business and move from the ideas stage to the start up stage and beyond. Being truthful about these elements will help you keep your realistic head on rather than building a business based on pipe dreams and unachievable ideals.

Below is a basic SWOT table for you to fill in. I have started you off with some suggestions. In general, Strengths and Weaknesses are internal factors whereas Opportunities and Threats tend to be external factors.

Strengths	Weaknesses
What are your Unique Selling Points (USP)? Do you have resources available to you such as experts or facilities?	Are there areas where you lack the necessary skills? What things may hinder your success? Do you have insufficient funds to harness opportunities?
Opportunities	**Threats**
List current trends and emerging technologies you could exploit to your advantage. E.g. there might be a rise in Government funding for childcare or a competitor may have gone out of business.	The state of the economy, changes in technology the strength of the competition; these can all be real threats to your business.

This table can be included in your business plan or elements of it used as appropriate throughout the plan. Some people choose not to add the more negative aspects into plans when others will be viewing it. This is your choice, but experience tells me that honesty with lenders and supporters of your business is always key. Lies or omissions from the plan may be glaringly obvious to them and they will question you on them, or they may crop up in the future if things are not going so well and they will feel deceived. It is far better to outline where your weaknesses or threats are upfront and explain exactly what you intend to do about them.

In her business plan, Lucy decided not to add in anything about her lack of ability to work full time or mention that her hours would be decreased over the summer months when the children were off school. She didn't see it as important. However, when the summer came around and the bills needed paying, Lucy had to return to the bank and ask for an overdraft. The bank had seen the business plan and couldn't understand what had gone wrong. Was business not going so well?

When Lucy explained she had to take off time to care for the children over the summer therefore reducing her income and her ability to pay back her start up loan and other bills, the bank was not amused as this crucial factor hadn't been made clear to them from the outset. Much negotiation followed and Lucy was thankfully able to sort it out. However, honesty up front would have served her better. The bank may now have a different view of her and her business in the future as her credibility took a blow.

Lucy didn't mean to be dishonest or mislead the banks, but it could have cost her everything. Don't make the same mistake. Keep your plan simple to read, transparent and realistic. Get someone else to read your business plan and give you some honest feedback before you show it to possible investors. All too often I have seen badly written, poorly spelt and terribly presented business plans expecting investors to put in large amounts of money and trust. Would you trust someone who couldn't clearly explain what their business does or how it will be run?

A final word on business plans. It's important to review your business plan every three months. It should not be set in stone. Your business plan can and should be an evolving document which you add to as your ideas and business grows. Revisiting it regularly helps you to refocus on your business and ensure you are keeping on track.

REVIEW OF CHAPTER EIGHT

- Give planning the time and attention to detail it deserves.

- Writing a business plan will start to make things more real.

- During the business planning stage, be honest and realistic.

- Remember your personal success targets and your personal commitments and values and ensure they are reflected and considered in your business plan.

- Make sure your business plan is professional and presented well if you expect others to take your idea seriously.

- Help persuade investors and yourself that your business is truly viable and worth investing time and money in. Do plenty of research so you can back up your statements with hard data and real feedback.

- Ensure that you clearly define your marketplace, customers and growth potential. Be aware of competitive advantages and threats. Use SWOT analysis and focus groups to help.

- Review your business plan regularly to help you stay on track and shift your strategy accordingly if necessary.

- Don't forget the basics: Include your contact details and product details. Remember to write this as if it is for someone who knows nothing about you, your business and the sector in which you are planning to trade.

- Be strong on your financials – know how much you need to start, run and grow the business. Use professionals if you are unable to keep accurate records yourself.

CHAPTER NINE - SECURING CUSTOM

By now you have a clear idea of your business, what it will be and how it will run. You have also considered the financial aspects of the business along with who your customers and your competition are. It's therefore time to start thinking about how your potential customers will find your business and how to persuade them to buy from you.

Over the years I have worked with many business owners who forgot about this part of the start-up process. Many of them naively thought that merely opening the business, be it an office or shop, would bring customers to them. Alas, if only business was that easy! Not only do you need to have a fantastic offering – a brilliant value proposition that customers will love... you also need to shout about it from the rooftops in whichever way you are able to.

Certainly, merely having a business name, stationery, a shop or stock does not make you into a business. A business needs paying-customers as you are not really in business until money is coming in. I really do wish it was as easy as setting up a website with a shopping trolley or telling a few friends you have started your business. However, getting your business out there into the marketplace takes time and effort. Without this effort your business is unlikely to last very long.

The first ingredient involved in successfully marketing your business is *you*. In fact, you are the reason for this business and people will buy from you because you will be passionate about your business and believe in it and its products. Don't rely on others to market your business or sell your products, at least in the first instance. You need to do that yourself. As your business grows others will join your team publicising and selling, but you still need to inject your passion and belief into the team to ensure maximum marketing power.

We are bombarded with marketing messages every day: on the side of buildings, in e-mails, in adverts on the television, on labels on products and so the list goes on. Your job is to get your potential clients to notice you and your marketing. While this may sound daunting, with some sensible ideas, a strong brand identity, hard work and consistency, you can get your product out there in front of your potential customers.

You need an engaging and appealing brand name and logo to stand out from the crowd and get noticed. As such, the second ingredient for effective marketing is your brand. The more times we see a name or brand the more we are likely to associate with it and consider buying it or from it. Most of my customers say they came across my work in more than one way before they decided to hire me as a coach or consultant. Some of us like to have a new company recommended to us by a trusted friend, maybe meet the owner at a business networking event and then see their product advertised in a magazine before we decide to buy from them.

CHOOSING YOUR MARKETING TOOLS

Let's be realistic, your new business is not going to be able to afford to compete with big companies when it comes to getting your product known. Unless you have really big investors (and equally big budgets) you won't be able to afford to throw huge amounts at promoting your wares. Big companies like car manufacturers or breweries can afford to spend huge amounts of money on product placement and sponsorship, whereby consumers constantly see the brand or product name in their daily lives. Small businesses, particularly start-ups need to be a little more imaginative while marketing on a shoestring budget. So it's important to select the right tools and the right targets.

Marketing is about much more than placing some fancy adverts in glossy magazines. There are many places to target your marketing messages; from your own website and brochure to business cards, posters, leaflets and flyers. You might even decide to stage an open day or a launch party to generate publicity. Consider anything which will help get your name out there and make people aware of your business and what it offers. It is easy to get carried away at this point and spend far too much money on activities which are not likely to help bring in customers. Think carefully before you spend time and money on marketing. Think back to your marketplace research and your findings regarding how your demographic audience buys and why they buy. This will help shape your marketing messages (what you say) and where you place them.

Think for a few minutes how you could get some form of communication out to the public about you, your products and your company and which audience you'd be communicating with. Use the table below to list ways in which you could communicate with your target audience.

Form of Communication	Target Audience
e.g. Article in local paper (PR)	potential clients
e.g. Spot in local radio (PR)	potential clients, raising awareness of your expertise
e.g. Attendance at business networking events	Other small business owners who might recommend you to potential clients

PUBLIC RELATIONS

Public Relations (PR) looks at the way in which you develop and maintain relationships with the public outside of your business. The public is made up of different groups on which your business depends in order for it to be a success. Therefore it may include customers, investors, the press, employees, the community in which you trade and so on. PR, both good and bad, can be very powerful and can positively or adversely affect your business and its ultimate success.

Publicity can be about raising awareness of one particular product or event or the whole brand. Used well, PR can help you build brand awareness and gain higher credibility. However, this can take far too much time and money for you to compete at the same levels as the big PR agencies. Whilst you can pay for PR or make use of a PR agency in the early days, it is likely that you will need to arrange your own PR and be a little creative to get yourself noticed. However, some quality targeted PR can be valuable to you. In my experience, PR tends to come in three main categories:

- PR for you the business owner
- PR for the business
- PR for the products.

PR FOR YOU THE BUSINESS OWNER

Let's consider first your PR. This business is yours, you developed it and manage it and therefore people are invariably buying from you during the initial stages of a business either directly (as they meet you in a sales meeting) or indirectly (as they may have heard about you and your business and decide they would like to buy from you). Many of us bought items from the Body Shop because we knew Anita Roddick was trying to make a difference and establish something unique. Most of us never met her but we knew her story and vision. She was the personification of her brand; she drove the company and most of the PR focused on her, her vision, beliefs, values, achievements and her activism rather than the products.

If you can find ways to get yourself well-known in relation to a particular product, such as Anita Roddick when it came to certain topics (the beauty industry, entrepreneurship, fair trade, the environment and human rights activism) you can generate many column inches and be called upon by the media to talk about your areas of expertise.

What makes you unique? Note down here anything about you that makes you unique or interesting.	Who would be interested in your story Note down here who would be interested in this?
e.g. a woman in a male industry	e.g. Industry press, general press

For instance, I get asked to speak on the radio and TV about women in the workplace and business. I often don't get paid but the publicity this provides in raising my profile and cementing in people's minds the work I do is valuable. However, it's not simple. To start with you need a level of credibility before you are invited to speak and, when you do, you need to make sure you come across well or the PR can produce a more negative then positive result.

PR FOR THE BUSINESS AND PRODUCTS
PR for a particular item, product or service can also be gained by distributing press releases, giving out free samples in your shop or local high street, or by having a launch event or a taster day. Be creative. Seek out something which will help you gain some press coverage and get people interested in and talking about your product. You don't have a big budget so think quality rather than quantity. Gordon Ramsey regularly takes to the street with samples when trying to help failing restaurant owners, his idea being if they won't come to you then you need to go to them. Of course having Gordon by your side helps gain some interest and publicity. But it's a great idea. In fact, can you think of any celebrities who might endorse your product? Sally, the founder of Babylicious frozen

baby food famously wrote to Victoria Beckham after meeting her mother-in-law at The Baby Show exhibition.

TOP TIPS TO GENERATE GOOD PR

- **Target local newspapers and TV news programmes.** Try and get some free editorial coverage in your local paper about your business or on your local news programme. Find an interesting angle. Perhaps you've had your one hundredth customer since opening two months ago and gave them a free shopping spree, or perhaps the company has won an award, or you are staging a local taste session for your wedding cakes. Free editorial works better than advertising and costs nothing (other than the time it takes to write and send in a press release or phone a newsdesk and send in a photo).

- **Target national publications**, especially industry specific magazines if your story has wider appeal. The press love "female business owner in a man's world" type stories or "backroom to boardroom business growth" stories, such as the Woolworths manager who re-opened her closed store as Wellworths. However, be careful that the angle they give the story is positive for your business.

- **Write articles** on your specific area of expertise or create an online blog to raise the profile and credibility of you, your business and your products. You can post your articles all over the web and submit to publications, all of whom are desperate for content, particularly if it is free to use. Make sure you include your contact information and web address on every article you distribute. Blog owners are frequently invited as experts to contribute to features, news programmes and the like.

- **Offer your product/service for free** as a giveaway/competition to targeted publications. This is another way to gain some free editorial coverage without spending out on advertising.

- **Network!** Getting out and about, networking and meeting people will play a big part in your brand awareness exercise and will often open doors to other forms of business promotion and sales. Over the many years I have been in business I have relied heavily on networking, meeting people and forging connections. Whilst it can be time consuming, it has led to some great collaborations, meeting wonderful people and making some new friendships and business partnerships. It's also a way of keeping yourself sane, as business ownership can be a lonely thing at times. Look out for women's networks, industry specific networks, online networks and those arranged by organisations such as the chambers of trade or commerce and enterprise agencies. Online networks provide a great way to get yourself well-known and interact with like-minded people without having to go out and spend time meeting people face-to-face. As you get better known among the communities in which you participate - you will find people start to refer business your way.
- **Gather testimonials and ask customers for referrals.** Once you have some happy customers willing to share their experiences, make the most of this. Customer-led marketing can be a great way of marketing your business. Simply ask your happy customers to provide you with a testimonial and ask them if they know of anyone else who'd be interested in your service. You might even offer rewards or commission for their referred business.
- Ensure that each piece of marketing literature you use includes a call to action. Tell your customers exactly what they should do next. On your website – 'click here to find out more'; on your business card: 'call this number for a free consultation' and in your press releases and adverts 'visit www.xyz.com'.

ADVERTISING

Advertising can be one of the quickest ways of giving away your money. Adverts can cost from a few hundred pound to thousands of pounds depending on the publication. You will also need to pay a designer to set out the advert and ensure that it is a professional advert which presents the right message to your audience.

If you do decide to advertise, find out the readership demographic of different publications and websites to ensure they fit the needs of your business before even considering paying for advertisements. Don't pay for anything which does not directly reach your target audience.

When Lucy started her PR business she decided she would need to advertise in her local paper and local business magazine to find some new clients. She told me how each advert presented its own problems: from design, size, and layout issues to a whole host of publication-led mistakes such as printing the wrong advert, publishing incorrect telephone numbers, poor quality print, and so on. In total, Lucy spent £4,000 on advertising in the first year. When I asked her how she got her clients during that year she admitted through networking and word of mouth referrals. In fact, she didn't know of a single person who came to her as a direct result of the adverts, although she wouldn't ever know if they had raised her profile or had some impact on people's decision to use her services. But what she did know was that she had generated £20,000 turnover in year one and wouldn't be spending so much on advertising in year two.

As Lucy discovered, the cost of advertising soon mounts up and there is no guarantee that it will bring you the returns you require. The effectiveness of advertising varies from business to business, so don't necessarily dismiss it out of hand as any business can benefit from good strategic advertising. When you consider advertising though, think carefully about the place in which your advert will appear and how you will be able to tell if it has had an impact. You can ask new customers where they found out about you, or include a voucher in an advert for them to bring in with them, this and other ways can help you monitor response rates to adverts.

Online advertising often generates better response and you can better track how many people clicked your ad and see where your customers are coming from if they click to your website from your advertising and marketing efforts. So about that…

USING THE INTERNET: HAVING A WEBSITE

Using the internet to publicise your business is generally a no-brainer. If you don't use the web, it's likely that your competitors will. Before you spend large amounts of hard earned cash on your website, consider how much business it is likely to bring in? Do you just need some well designed basic information pages with your contact details or a fully functioning online shopping experience?

It's important therefore to consider the following:
- How will you stand out from all the others on the Internet?
- How will people find you? How will you promote your site? And what will make people visit your website?
- How will you use your Internet presence to make you money and benefit your business? What essentially will your website be used for? Will it be a way of directing people to visit your high street shop? Will people be able to buy directly from you online? Or will your website

simply act as an online brochure, providing information to enhance your business and provides potential customers with all the information they need?

- How involved do you want to be in setting up your website and editing it?

1. **STEP ONE: Select a web address.** To start with you need to select a website address or domain name. If your company sells baby clothes and is called "Designer baby" you may find the web address has already been bought by someone else, so you might need to change your domain name to suit. For example changing it to 'designer baby world' might better enable you to register that domain name, if it is available.

Buying the domain name is not that difficult or expensive, although you will need to renew the registration and there is a small fee attached to that. I always recommend that, if the web address using your company name or brand is available, you buy it now. Even if you can't afford or don't have the time to set up a website, at least you know you have the address rather than someone else.

Once you have purchased a domain name you will need to find a web host to host the site. Website hosting is often done in conjunction with your design work and the company who has handled that aspect of your web site will usually arrange an annual fee for hosting your site.

2. **STEP TWO: Set up your e-mail address.** When you own a web domain name, you will also be able to arrange web forwarding from the domain name. That will mean you don't have to be Sheila@freemail.com, rather you will be Sheila@mybusinessname.com. Freemail addresses don't inspire confidence as they

don't look very professional and people can wonder just how successful or established you really are. Other internet services you may consider could e-mail marketing campaign providers. You can use sites such as www.graphicmail.com to handle mailing out to databases of contacts, getting people to sign up for regular e-mail contact and sending newsletters, or ask your web design company if they can add extra services to your site.

3. **STEP THREE: Decide whether to design your own site or outsource to a professional company.** Many small business owners design their own site. I'm sure we have all visited home made websites that have clearly used free downloadable software to do the designing. Whilst doing it yourself is the cheaper option, be careful about the level of professionalism of the site and how that reflects back on you and your business.

4. **STEP FOUR:** Find a web designer and developer to suit your needs. Good web designers don't need to cost the earth and will set up the look and feel of your site. Look at your competitors' websites, ask other business owners who they used to design and develop their website, note down websites that you like the look of, then get quotes from at least three web designers against a specification you have drawn up.

5. **STEP FIVE: Keep your website fresh and up to date at all times,** otherwise it's neither professional nor an effective marketing tool. Badly designed and out of date websites can do more harm than having no website at all. Depending on the arrangements you have with your web designers, it can be possible for you to update, change or modify your site without the need to keep paying them each time.

Many women I know in business choose to only have a single holding page during the early stages of business until they are sure what they need on their site or because they don't have the time or money to develop a really good site. Others choose to pay for a mini site within someone else's site.

Just consider these following questions; will having a website help my business? Do my competitors have websites? Is it worth the investment? How professional will it look? Can I afford to have a website? And, perhaps more importantly, can I afford not to have one?

E-COMMERCE

Your website may have an e-commerce element to it. That is some way of people selecting and paying for goods online. Some people successfully run their business using payment platforms such as Paypal and by having an e-bay account. E-bay is not to be sniffed at, with over 181 million customers worldwide, 10 million in the UK. In Britain alone there are up to three million items on sale every day. Running your business on e-bay can be a way of getting started without any large overheads or expenses. Just be aware that e-bay take a cut of all transactions and charge listing fees. However this is marginal compared to the cost of having your own website. It's a case of weighing up the pros and cons.

It may be that you need your own website with an e-commerce element. Speak to other business owners who have sites which use a solution you think would work for your business. Discuss your needs with a web company and work out the best way for you and your business.

HOW WILL PEOPLE FIND YOU ON THE INTERNET?

Just putting up a website with a fancy shopping cart and some pretty pictures will not bring you in customers and sales. You will need to attract visitors to your site. When people type "secretarial services" into a search engine, will your virtual office assistant company come up in its search listings? And, if so, how far down the list are you? Are you ranked at the top of page one or at the bottom of page eight? Some businesses can carry out search engine optimisation on your website, making it come higher up the search engine rankings. Depending on your business and its uniqueness, the success of this will vary. For example, if you have a very niche business, such as AnythingLeftHanded.co.uk, or minimal competition, you will most likely appear high up in the search results.

You can also consider pay-per-click adverts on search engines. These are usually shown at the top or highlighted down the side of a ranked search. You basically bid for keywords that are relevant to your website/business and pay when someone clicks on your ad. The value and success of these campaigns vary from business to business. One successful business lady I know has a limit of £1 a day on her pay per click so once a £1 has been reached her advert is no longer shown. This way she keeps a control of the budget and £30 a month is not much in comparison to the amount she spends on other marketing materials and campaigns.

Some business owners believe the better connected their website is to others, the more visitors they have to their site. Having mutual links to their site on other peoples sites, having a presence on websites like 'Linked in', Facebook, and Twitter with links back to your site can all help in driving traffic to your site.

Once you have visitors on your site you then need to work out how to capture their details so you can remain in contact with them and how to change them from browser to buyer. Some people provide free downloadable publications or free samples in exchange for visitors filling out a form containing their contact information. Some offer subscription to an e-newsletter or entry into a free prize draw.

SELLING

The truth is, if there are no sales, you don't really have a business. All too often I hear of people with a business idea which looks fine on paper, they have spent years developing it and thousands of pounds, (some even re-mortgaging their house) but, as yet they have few or even no customers. Often this comes down to poor research or poor selling. Indeed there are many people out there who have a great well-researched business idea but they find it difficult to sell. Many women often tell me they don't like selling, or it's not their thing. Unfortunately it's very hard to build a successful business without actually having to sell. While word-of-mouth and other methods of marketing are focused on the brilliance of the product rather than the involvement of the owner in the marketing process, few products sell themselves in enough numbers to make you and your business a success, no matter how amazing your product is.

If you don't like selling consider how you will overcome that or else you may need to reconsider if running a business is really for you.

Even if you have sold in the past you will now need to learn how to sell to your particular audience. This may be different to how you have sold before and require a different approach.

You may find it difficult to make your first sales. Who do you speak to? How do you approach them? Should you cold call by examining your customer profile and picking up the phone to speak to those who fit it? Or should you seek introductions? Consider drawing on existing contacts, people you know socially and professionally, family and friends. Can they introduce you to people who would be interested in buying from you? Could you have an open day or a party to launch the business and get the sales ball rolling? Could you ask everyone you speak to during the selling process if they can recommend anyone who might be interested in what you are offering?

So far we've looked at who your target market is, how they buy and how you will find them and get yourself and your products in front of them. Now you need to consider their needs, what benefits they are seeking and, ultimately, what will encourage them to part with their cash. Equally, what could put them off?

Pitching and selling needs advance thought. Think about the words you will use, how you will describe your product, relay its benefits and suggest reasons why your prospective customer should consider buying it. Practice a short but informative presentation, take samples with you if you can and provide prospective customers with the knowledge and information they need to make an informed decision about buying from you.

A good sales-person needs in-depth knowledge of the product, confidence in themselves, along with belief in and enthusiasm for their product. They also need to know when to stop talking and actually ask for the sale. People often buy because of the person selling and the way in which they make them feel. It's a well versed business phrase that 'people buy from people.' Think about the last time you bought an item. Did the sales person make a difference? Did they put you off buying from them or did they convince you to do the deal?

Once you have a few sales under your belt, your confidence will increase and word of mouth soon travels. If people like what they bought from you they will tell others. Ask for help from others to get your name out there. Accept however that selling a new idea, business or product takes hard work and you will get knock-backs, but that's all part of running a business. You need to learn how to get back up and start again. Sales will come but you need to be persistent.

TOP SALES TIPS

- Be professional and be yourself. We regularly buy the person as much as the product, so think about why people will want to buy from you.
- Know and believe in your product. Be able to answer any questions and objections. Be enthusiastic and make the person you are selling to feel good about what you are offering.
- Focus on benefits rather than features. For example: 'It will save you time and give you back that half an hour you would usually spend on performing a certain task and enable you to sit back and relax.' would work better than telling someone. 'The product has a fully adjustable extending widget'.
- Remember to ask for the sale! Lots of people forget to ask if someone would actually like to make the purchase. I remember spending 30 minutes once with a sales lady for a recruitment company who I had called to come and see us. I had already done the research I knew I needed to use their services. I knew they offered about the best price but she still gave me the whole sales pitch. When she had completed her pitch she put away her brochures and thanked me for my time. About to leave I asked her did she want to sell to me or not? All I needed from her was the question. 'Are you ready to do business with us?' Asking for business and making follow up calls after initial enquiries can increase your sales, so don't put it off; if someone has contacted you about your products they expect you will try and sell to them. They are a hot and qualified lead, so make the most of them.

- Get feedback. Find out why someone might not be interested at this moment in time and what might make them more interested. You can then use this when you follow them up or to tweak your sales pitch for the next customer.
- Make sure what you are offering satisfies customers' unmet needs. Listen to what those needs are by asking questions and gathering feedback about your products and services. Listen.
- Use happy customers as an extension of your own sales force. Ask them for testimonials, referrals and case studies. Have them share their positive experiences with prospective customers.
- Keep in touch with customers regularly. It's far easier to sell to existing customers than it is to find new ones. The fact is, if someone has bought from you once it's likely that they will buy from you again. As long as the first experience was a positive one.

Talking of happy customers… in the next chapter let's look in more detail at how to keep customers happy with good customer communication and high quality customer service.

Review of Chapter Nine

- Know who your target market is and how to find them. Half the battle is getting in front of potential customers. Consider how your potential customers will find your business and how to persuade them to buy from you.

- Think about how your brand and business image will encourage people to buy from you.

- Choose your marketing tools and messages wisely. Consider using various methods of getting yourself, your company and products in front of your target audience.

- Try to build up your credibility as an expert in your field, look for newsworthy PR angles and think creatively about how to raise brand awareness through competitions, events, endorsements and networking activities.

- Consider the bigger picture when creating a web presence: from how you will stand out and keep your site fresh to how people will find your website.

- Selling is vital to any business. If you don't like selling, consider developing your sales skills through a training course or other professional support.

- Create a strong benefit-rich sales pitch. Always ask for a sale and give calls to action, both in your marketing literature and when selling face-to-face.

- Listen to what your customers' needs are so you can ensure that you: a) fulfil those needs and b) provide a product/service that generates sales by word of mouth recommendation.

CHAPTER TEN – KEEPING CUSTOMERS HAPPY AND LOYAL

Customer Care should be at the very heart of your business, right from your customers' very first experience of you. Be aware of the experience your customer has when buying from you, how it makes them feel and whether it is likely to encourage them to recommend you to others.

Working with happy customers will make life so much easier for you. Put in the effort to give your customers an excellent experience; it will be well worth it.

Nicky knew that keeping the parents at her crèche happy would be key to gaining new customers. She decided from the start to put the parents needs central to decisions she made about the structure and management of the crèche. So, as well as considering the needs of the children and the staff, she also kept in mind at all times how the parents' needs could be considered. Nicky found that spending time every week talking to the parents as they dropped off and collected the children was a valuable way of keeping up to date with their needs. She also learnt that pinning up notes or sending letters home didn't always work, so introduced technology such as text updates and a web site which parents could log into and find out about activities and events. This worked much better.

Nicky always consults her customers before making changes, adding new products and services and making changes to management within the crèche. Keeping the customers at the heart of the business has made Nicky's job much easier and more enjoyable while making the selling process much easier, as her happy customers recommend her business to others.

Reselling the same thing to established customers, selling a different product to the same customers, upselling and keeping your customers happy so they return and recommend you to others, should be in your mind from the day you start your business, not when sales have slumped and you don't know how to attract new customers.

Keep things professional when dealing with customers.
- Ensure that all written materials have a professional look and are accurate, including spelling and grammar. Consider everything from press releases, marketing leaflets, websites, signs in your shop window, menus on the table, invoices, e-mails and letters.
- Consider ways in which you can make your business look more serious without huge investment. For example, rather than using your home address, can you use a mailbox or a PO Box?
- Be approachable. Make it easy for your customers to find you and communicate with you. Keep communication clear.
- Ensure communication remains true to your brand and brand values.
- Have a good Customer Relationship Management System (CRM) to ensure that customer relationships are consistent. Should a key member of staff leave you should be able to tell who's been dealing with a particular customer or problem so that a new recruit should be able to pick up interaction from where they left off.

- Record each customer contact so anyone who deals with a particular customer is aware of responses, what's been said and purchased in the past, feedback and dates of communications.
- Remember to include your contact details on all communication: e-mail footers, appointment cards, flyers, discount vouchers should all include your web address, telephone number and branding.
- Keep it legal. When you are running a business you'll need to store information about your customers so that you can communicate with them. Mailing lists, databases, records of purchases and so on are all normal things for businesses to retain. However, in order to store this information, you must not only comply with the data protection regulations, but you also need to register with the Data Protection Registrar.

HANDLING COMPLAINTS

Be ready for complaints. Make sure you have considered exactly how you will handle them before they even happen. This will help you cope if it ever happens. Set up a quick and simple procedure to handle complaints and concerns. What should you say? What actions should be taken? What checks should be made? What can you do to go the extra mile to turn a complainer into an evangelist of your products/services?

Turning an unhappy customer into a happy customer is hugely beneficial. Not only does it prevent the negative PR that an unhappy customer can generate; if you win a customer back, they are likely to repay you with their loyalty. You will also find that considering areas of possible complaints can highlight areas of weakness that you need to concentrate on. Try using your website or visiting your shop as if you were a customer. Do you have a good experience or could things be improved upon? Consider your customers' point of view. Your goal is not only to deliver on customer expectations but to exceed them.

PERSONAL REPRESENTATION

You represent your business and, as an individual, your image is the representation of you that others see. Your image should be one that you feel comfortable and confident with. It should reflect your better qualities, be genuine and sincere and not slick, phoney or over-rehearsed. In an ideal world people would judge us on our performance alone and not on how we look. However, in the real world of work, image and confidence are deemed as important aspects of our suitability for promotion, winning that contract, getting better projects, encouraging a contractor to trust and buy from us. And, importantly, first impressions really do count.

The way you behave, your body language and the way you dress can all impact on your success as a business owner. It is no secret that the majority of communication is non-verbal. You need to feel comfortable in yourself, how you present yourself and how you act. You also need to present an image that is suitable for the people you are meeting and dealing with. When you are attending meetings therefore, there are some simple rules to consider. Always:

- Arrive on time
- Be prepared
- Look the part
- Follow up.

Think now about the way you behave and the image you project. Are your behaviour and image suitable for the business you are in and the type of people you will be doing business with?

Review of Chapter Ten

- Whether you are turning a hobby into a business or starting up a large company, you still need to run a professional business.

- Ensure that customer care is a priority.

- Consider your customers' experience from their point of view. Have empathy. Always strive to exceed expectations and improve the experience.

- Be open and approachable. Listen to feedback and act on it.

- Maintain a high level of professionalism across every point of contact: from written materials to face-to-face contact.

- Have a good CRM system where all customer interaction and communication is recorded and accessible to all those who deal with customers.

- Pay attention to detail.

- Go the extra mile when it comes to handling complaints and be sure you have processes in place to deal with them effectively.

- Think about the image you and your business portray to customers. Present yourself professionally. Be punctual, well-dressed and well-prepared, always.

CHAPTER ELEVEN - CREATE A SUPPORT NETWORK

Starting up your first business can be physically and emotionally draining. Trying to do everything on your own can be unrealistic too. There is nothing wrong with having help from others to get your business into the market place and trading. You need to decide for yourself what type of help you will need at the various stages of business development. It's worth reviewing Chapter Five where we discussed your skills and identify the areas in which you need some support; i.e. fill the gaps in your own skill set and capabilities. For example, if you're uncertain about the financial aspects of the business, working with an experienced book keeper or accountant to gain their advice would be a suitable solution.

Ultimately, all business owners need a support network of some kind. This could be a group of like-minded business people: a business coach, mentor or someone working in your sector. Or it could consist of people who are at arm's length from the business itself, such as family and friends. Many areas have business networking groups for women in business now and these can be a great source of support, as well as providing a platform for you to gain and share skills and knowledge.

FAMILY AND FRIENDS
Family and friends can offer you lots of support during the lifecycle of your business – from start up to exit. Some aspects of running a business can be isolating and there may be times you wish to talk to someone about the business who is not involved directly with it; someone who you trust to keep your

conversations confidential. Family and close friends are likely to fit the bill here.

I have found that the women in business I work with like to have someone they can talk to about their ideas; someone who can act as a sounding block. Lots of new business owners find they need someone they can trust to bounce ideas off, both for feedback and just to work through things by expressing themselves and articulating their thoughts. This enables them to gain from other people's experiences as well as feeling less alone with their work.

Having someone you can turn to for support during business start-up can be a huge help. Consider carefully what such a person can actually help you with and how involved you want them to be in your journey. Also, importantly, consider how involved they are willing to be.

Support can be physical or emotional. Physically, members of your support network may actually be able to perform physical tasks for you in order to help you and the business. It's not unknown for family and friends to pitch in for free in the early stages of a new business, helping with packing items for postage, making goods, serving customers and helping with specific skills like website design, accountancy or marketing. Alternatively, they might be able to offer their time to help you out by carrying out tasks which are not business-oriented, such as helping with childcare, doing chores around the home or pitching in to help with other commitments you may have, therefore helping free your time to devote on the business, whilst easing your workload and reducing your stress levels.

Emotional support is commonly provided by a network of close family and friends; particularly when it comes to helping to build your confidence. (Remember confidence is one of the keys to success).

However, you should think carefully whether to tell family and friends about your decision to go self-employed and whether revealing your business plans to them will be beneficial to you. Only you know your family. Quite often family and friends will try to put you off. Usually this is due to them being worried about your welfare. As such, don't automatically expect family and friends to understand your passion for your business, nor your willingness to work so hard. They are often concerned for you and your health, so will try to get you to be realistic about your business, often questioning its likely success, suggesting you be sensible and slow down.

This can come across as if they don't have confidence in you or the business, but it's more likely that they don't understand your desire to make this business a success and don't share your vision. All they can see is you working hard and making sacrifices, so they have a limited viewpoint, whereas you see the bigger picture. That said, it can be worth having people to play devil's advocate as it provides you with a bigger picture. This gives you the opportunity to consider alternative opinions and prove your points.

Many business owners have told me that they don't tell their family members about the business as they usually give inappropriate advice. Some families are too encouraging and provide a blinkered view on the potential success of your business, while others are more likely to try and dissuade you from starting a business, telling you it will never work and you would be better getting a job. By the way, my family still ask me when I will get a job even though I have been self employed almost all of my adult life!

My mum still hasn't accepted that customers call me sometimes when I'm "not working". This could mean I'm having a coffee with her or have just collected the children from school. If people call within reasonable office hours then

I will always take the call, regardless. Customers don't know that you have decided for the first time in weeks to take a morning off, or that your daughter has a dental appointment. Anyway, you have a choice now with mobile phones whether you want to answer the call or put them through to voice mail.

Mums often don't see this however. They only see their daughter trying to do too much. Consequently they may not offer the best business advice.

Self employment is very different from being employed and, if your family and friends have no experience of working for themselves, it will be hard for them to understand you, your worries and your joys at starting your new business.

Bearing all of this in mind, only you can decide whether to involve your family or friends in your business support network. In some cases having them to talk to about your business or to provide physical or emotional support can be fantastic. In other cases it's better to keep work and personal life entirely separate and not discuss business with family and friends at all. That way they can provide you with a welcoming world in which you can escape from business.

CAN FAMILY BE STAFF?
You may decide to have family working for you on the payroll. I am often asked my opinion of this and it's very difficult to know how to answer, as it very much depends on the individuals concerned. Many husband and wife teams work well together and seem to be able to keep their personal and business relationships separate (although the occasional discussions about what to do about a particular client or opportunity may surface at the breakfast table).

I also know of businesses where mums, sisters, brothers in-law and children are all working in the business. These family run businesses can be very successful. Their success usually comes down to good strong relationships built on trust, communication and a clear understanding of what is expected of everyone. Families are certainly very honest with each other and probably less diplomatic than they might be with non-related members of staff (which of course has its pros and its cons).

I recommend that, if you do have family and/or friends working for you, you keep things reasonably formal, with suitable contracts (employment, partnership and so on) and in a legal manner i.e. paying them above minimum wage salaries and tax. This should help avoid difficulties in the future as they may be willing to work for nothing during the start up phase but what happens if you grow and have a good level of income or have even other paid staff? What will they expect then? Will they expect the same salary as others? Will they expect back pay to when they started? Or are they just going to be pleased to see you grow and expand and happy to have been able to contribute their time?

If you do choose to work with family or friends:
- Set expectations early on as you don't want to fall out with family or friends over business related issues. Expectations can change and the lack of clarity of expectations and money can lead to difficulties both in the business and the family.
- Formalise your working relationship with appropriate contracts.
- Consider what will happen over the long-term. If family and friends can only work for a while, how will you manage when they can't help out any more and you now have to pay someone? Or what would you do if you rely on a family member and they become ill or unable to carry on helping you? How will this affect you, them and the business?

One woman business owner I know works very closely with her mum. When she started her business she needed an injection of cash. Her mum was not only willing to invest the money for start up, but also to work in the business. As mum and daughter both put money in and both worked full time in the business, a formal agreement was made right at the beginning about what was expected from each of them and how the ownership was split. The daughter actually owns the majority share and takes a larger salary, as the business requires her expertise. However, as this was agreed up front, both are happy with the situation and it isn't necessary to discuss it on a regular basis. As with any partnership or collaboration, it's important that each party benefits in some way and feels good about what's happening – a win-win situation is what you should always strive for, as in the case above.

Over the years I have watched many women start-up a business with help and support from family and friends. It's only natural to do so and most find it works well for them with few problems. Yet, for others, things can go very wrong and have an impact not only on the business but on their relationship with that person and often the whole family. As such, some people feel that mixing family/friendships and working relationships are not worth the risk of damaging those relationships.

When Joy established her salon, her daughter was on maternity leave and offered to help out with the paperwork from home. Initially this worked well and both mother and daughter enjoyed working together. Joy's daughter then decided not to return to her full time job and turned to her mother for additional work to bring in the income she had lost. Joy had never envisaged having someone more than a few hours a week helping with the administration side of the

186

business which, in fact, Joy was capable of doing herself. However, as she wanted to help her daughter out and didn't want to let her down, she offered her more hours than the business needed. This quickly became an issue.

Joy was having to pay her daughter more than the business could really afford and this led to arguments and upset both in the business and the family. Expectations and long-term plans had not been clearly established from the outset.

Be aware that working in the business is likely to affect your current relationship with the person involved and this can often lead to arguments within the wider family unit, as Joy soon discovered. In fact, Joy's son became disgruntled that his mum was effectively paying his sister over the odds for work she didn't really need her to be doing, while his sister felt their mum was not paying her enough as she had bills to pay. These types of issues are often seen in family businesses where things have not been made clear from the beginning about what is and what isn't deemed as acceptable (hours, behaviour, payment, and so on).

OTHER BUSINESS OWNERS
You may be surprised just how much help other business owners will be willing to freely provide new business start ups with. Ask a business owner to be a mentor and you will be surprised how many are willing to give you some time for free so they can share their business experience with you.

If your business is likely to be selling to other businesses then developing good long term links with other business owners in your area will be particularly valuable to you. Networking can be a really valuable way of getting to know other business owners, learning from their experience, getting answers to questions and finding solutions to problems.

Networks are essentially groups of people or businesses who connect together for a purpose, either to promote themselves and their business, gain knowledge or share resources. They are often specific to a particular need, such as local business networks, female business networks or networks that are specific to a business sector such as IT networks and tourism groups. Networks can meet in person or online so look around for ones which suit you and your needs. Try ecademy.com or Linked-in; both offer online business networking.

Talking to other business owners about their experiences can be immensely helpful and offer you support during a time when you may be feeling alone and out of your depth. Hearing from others about their experiences can help build your confidence and knowledge. The quickest way to find business owners is via networks, so speak to your local Chamber of trade or economic development department or visit the Business Link website to find out about networks in your area.

As well as providing much-needed support, guidance and advice, networks can also be great for business. You will often make new contacts with buyers, suppliers and people who can support you in your business plans. You often find at network meetings that people are willing to share their knowledge and experiences, often through presentations and discussions. Building relationships with other business owners can lead to other benefits. Bartering and exchanging services and products can be a huge benefit to new business owners. Furthermore, contacts you make at networks will often refer business your way or provide you with the link in the chain to a service, solution or new recruit that you are seeking.

PROFESSIONAL SUPPORT

Most businesses buy in professional services at some time or another, from marketing, PR and payroll, to accounting, IT, design, business consultancy, training and legal advice. If you need to start buying in professional support, the costs can soon mount up.

If you're going to establish a Limited Company then it will be necessary to have an accountant. They will be able to help you with setting up a Limited Company, submitting Tax returns, sorting out PAYE (your payment system for staff) and carrying out annual accounts. Some will also help in developing business plans and financial plans. Selecting an accountant that suits you and your business is important and I recommend that you visit several accountants and talk to them about their services, what they can do for you and what experience they have of similar companies before choosing one. A good accountant will do more than just fill in your tax returns and you need to feel comfortable discussing your finances and business plans with them.

The combination of a good accountant and Bank Manager or business account manager from your bank can help you with sound business advice as well as having good connections to other business owners and up to date information which should be valuable to the growth of your business. As with the accountant, visit several banks and see which one suits you and your needs. Check out their charges and negotiate hard for a good deal.

If you have decided not to have a Limited Company you don't necessarily need an accountant. You will still need to keep up to date and accurate accounts and you may feel that you don't have the necessary skills to do this or that it's not the best use of your time. You could then consider using a book keeper that either works for you a few hours a week or a self employed book keeper who works as many hours as you need to keep your books in order.

We have already discussed the importance of marketing and PR in terms of getting you and your company out there. You may feel that you don't have the skills, contacts or time to do this effectively. There are many companies, freelancers and agencies which can provide you with support in these areas; from writing your publicity materials, and submitting articles to the press, to applying for awards and getting your business name out there in front of the correct audience.

As with all outsourced contracted services, you will find there are a variety of solutions, costs and different levels of support available and you need to speak to several companies before you decide which one suits you and your needs. Speak to other companies about who they use and what their experiences have been.

Using designers for your logo, website and general marketing materials may seem like a big investment but it can often be worth it if your business needs to have a professional brand image from the beginning. My first business logo was created on my second hand PC in a basic word processing package, as was my leaflet. I still have them and laugh now at the materials I was using in the mid 1990s but, at the time, they were fine. They served their purpose. They brought me in business and got me started. When the business was more established, I paid for a new logo and image to be designed. What I will never know is: If I had used that more professional image from the start, would my business have taken off quicker? That's what you will need to decide. Will you get a return on the investment you make in creating the right feel and look for your business from the outset?

If you visit your Local Enterprise Agency for support during business start-up, it is likely that they will offer you free support from a business advisor. A business advisor is someone who can help you in the planning and development of your business, reviewing your business plans and informing you about what financial support might be available in the form of grants and so on.

Finding a good business advisor can really make a difference. Many firms choose to contract a private business advisor (they are often freelance experienced business people) to help them at various stages of business start up, growth and during difficult periods. Having a person on hand to support you during these times enables you to develop a longer term relationship with someone who can help you work through the various stages of your personal and business growth. Their support is tailored to your ever-changing needs. A good mentor will also have a wealth of knowledge and experience to draw from and will be willing to share that with you in order to see you grow and develop.

As with all professions, you need to find someone who, not only has relevant experience, (make sure you ask them about their track record) but also understands your business needs and can advise you in the best way possible. Don't just settle for the first person you see, unless they understand your vision for your business.

For example, when Lucy set up her business she received free business support from an advisor who, having looked at her business idea and plans told her that it wouldn't work as there was far too much competition from established businesses out there. She was advised to re-consider her format. Lucy knew there was a gap in the market for smaller companies who often couldn't

afford the bigger PR firms. She carried on and found
another business advisor who gave her the support,
knowledge and confidence to keep going. Lucy is sure
that finding the right business advisor helped her during
her business start up.

DEVELOPING YOURSELF

Instead of calling in the professionals you may feel you can learn the skills you need in your business. There are many courses you can attend and books you can read to develop your own skills. Before you start your business and in the early stages look out for business start up and enterprise courses at your Local Enterprise Agency, college and through local private providers. Check they are going to cover the areas you need. There are also subject specific courses available such as basic accounting, business marketing, sales and staff management to mention just a few.

You will need to decide for yourself whether you would benefit from learning the skills yourself or if your time is better spent running the business and paying someone who already has the skills. I often find that the women I work with like to have a basic understanding of an area in the business even if they are going to get someone else to do the work. That way, they feel they understand at least a little bit about what they require.

RECRUITING STAFF

If you are planning to have staff, are you able to mange them? Do you know how to recruit, manage, train and retain staff? These are skills which can be learnt on a suitable course. Your local college, university or Enterprise Agency may offer courses for business owners recruiting their first staff members (some will also offer grants to help support the cost of employing your first team members).

There is much to consider, not only the legal side of employment, but also how to motivate staff and get the most from them.

When it comes to bringing people in to the business consider these few rules:

- Hire people who are not like you. There's no point hiring lots of people who share exactly the same interests and have the same skills just because you'll have lots to talk about. You need to fill the gaps so seek out people who complement your own areas of expertise rather than duplicating them.
- Devote a lot of time and effort to hiring the right people. A key fact of business is that people are the lifeblood of your business. They will help you drive your business toward success so don't just rush out a basic job ad, interview a few people and hire someone. Consider your needs carefully. Get to know people as well as you can at interview stage, including what motivates them and what their long-term personal ambitions are.
- Use your instincts. As well as basing your decisions to hire on a person's CV, demonstrable experience and references, go with your gut feeling.

REVIEW OF CHAPTER ELEVEN

- Figure out what type of help you will need at the various stages of business. Aim to fill the gaps in your own areas of expertise.

- Establish a support network consisting of those involved in business (mentors, professionals, other entrepreneurs) and those who aren't (friends and family). All business people need a sounding board external to the business.

- Seek out a blend of physical and emotional support.

- When working with family and friends in your business, make sure things are clear from the start about the expectations from both sides and keep things professional.

- Consider how much or how little involvement you want your friends and family to have in your business; whether you want to seek their support, advice or even employ them or whether you'd rather keep work and personal life separate.

- Find out how you can connect with other business owners via networks and develop those networks for long term business relationships. Gain support, guidance and advice, solutions, sales, referrals, services, supplies and friendships.

- Consider how bringing in the right professionals for the job can benefit your business, review what you need and what others can bring before parting with your hard earned cash.

- Don't forget to keep developing yourself and your skills where appropriate.

THE FUTURE OF YOUR BUSINESS

- WHERE NOW? WHAT NEXT?

CHAPTER TWELVE – WHAT NEXT?

The future should by now be looking pretty good. Whether you have already started your business or are still in the process of establishing it, you should now have an eye firmly on the future.

You've already sketched out a future vision for your business and considered what it will look like in two years, five years and even ten years from now. As we've discussed, it's worthwhile in the early stages of business ownership to consider what you would wish the future to look like, to have the end in mind.

When considering the next stages of your business's development and assessing your future, you should be evaluating:

1. Your long-term vision for the business and your final objective in terms of whether you'd pass it on, retire or sell the business, plus how fast you aim to achieve that end goal through expansion or other means.
2. How and when you intend to grow the business (organically, by raising capital, by setting up a franchise, etc)?
3. The implications and impact that the growth of your business will have on the business, its resources, on you, your time and your family commitments.
4. What you may need to do in order to cope with your growth plans, such as additional financial resources, staff, skills training and so on.

5. Whether your long-term plans still fit with your original reasons for starting your own business and fit with your desired lifestyle and level of commitment to work and family.

So let's elaborate on these points...

YOUR LONG-TERM VISION

Growing your business may be something you want to do or you might wish to keep it relatively small. This will of course depend on your personal ambition: "personal", being the key word here. Whatever you personally strive for is what is right for you and your business. Think about your long term commitment to the company. Do you want to run this business until you retire or is it just something for the next few years? Do you want to run it for a while and then let it fizzle out and get a job or do you wish to sell the business?

Any business, whatever its size, needs a committed owner. However in order to continue to be a success and move your business up a notch takes commitment, drive, persistence and ambition.

EXPANSION HOW AND WHEN? PLANNING, TIMING AND MANAGEMENT

If you wish to expand your business, start planning for it early on. Planning for your business growth needs to be an integral part of your overall business plan. If you are planning on changing from one shop to four shops then you will need more staff, your overhead costs will consequently increase and the way you manage the business is likely to change. You need to consider the impact of all of this on your business long before you expand so that you are prepared to cope effectively with expansion and successfully grow your business.

For example, business expansion may see you taking on bigger, more expensive premises, which adds a financial pressure on your business, but staying in premises which are unsuitable or too small can restrict the growth and flexibility of your business. Finding premises which provide you with the flexibility to grow will be vital to your plans and its worth considering this early on so you don't have to make several costly premises moves because you failed to plan ahead or think big over the long-term.

As well as planning, timing is also a key consideration. Don't grow too early. Ideally your business should be bursting at the seams before you expand, although don't wait until then to start planning for that growth. You should be able to anticipate growth long before you are in the 'bursting at the seams' position.

Another important consideration will be your ability to manage and lead a larger company than your current enterprise. Consider now what support and/or training will you need, whether you will need some personal development, such as some training in staff management, managing finances or raising capital, or whether you can recruit a director with expertise in growing businesses.

If you plan on developing your skills you will need to work out when you are going to have the time to come away from the business to do this. Many business owners find leaving the business to attend a course difficult as it not only costs them the course fees but they have to leave the business for its duration. However, not developing yourself can be a false economy as releasing time to gain training or having a coach come to you can give you an opportunity to reflect and gain a different perspective.

OTHER OPTIONS FOR BUSINESS GROWTH

Business growth doesn't have to be about opening new shops, getting more clients, selling more to the clients you already have or developing new products. There are some other possible routes to developing your business.

Setting up as a franchisee is just one of these. Now that you know how to set up and establish a business, it's worth asking yourself whether the model can be lifted and used in other areas of the country or world. This way other people just like you can start up their own business just like yours, but have your support and your knowledge (for which you will earn money).

I mentioned franchises earlier in the book as a way for you to start up in business. You may now like to revisit this section as a way to develop your personal business. The key rule with franchising and traditional business expansion is that, just as you can duplicate your successes, you can just as easily duplicate your mistakes, so make sure you have fine-tuned each area of your business before you grow or franchise it.

You will need to look into the legal structure and consider whether or not you'd feel comfortable with other people using your brand. You'll also need to consider how to ensure its integrity and quality remains true to your ideals and values.

As well as setting up a franchise based on your first business, there are other options you may wish to pursue. For example, you may decide to hire someone to run your first business and start up another business which is complementary to the one you already own, or a business which is a complete contrast, in order to give you variety.

Once her crèche was established and the staff were capable of running it without her help, Nicky began to

199

look at other businesses and ideas; first developing some barns on their farm to provide holiday accommodation and then opening a farm shop and café. Nicky now runs several businesses and still works from home most days to be there for her children. She has a busy life but Nicky says she wouldn't have it any other way.

WILL YOU STILL ENJOY IT WHEN YOU HAVE A BUSINESS EMPIRE?

It's crucial to ensure that any changes you make to your business still suit you and your family requirements. We spoke at length in Chapter Two about developing a business which suits you. It's important to keep revisiting this element of business ownership as it is easy to get carried away in the moment, expand the business, take on more staff and generally add to your workload and pressure. Think carefully about whether growing the business is something you want and are happy to do. It's far easier to keep a lid on growth plans for a while and grow organically or expand only when you are ready, than it is to expand and then be forced to cut back as you are finding the extra pressure more than you were willing to take on. Growing too quickly and having to reverse can kill a business.

All the time you are planning, developing and growing your business, you need to keep considering whether you will be able to manage the business and your lifestyle as it currently stands and as your business grows. There is likely to be an impact on you and your family as the business grows, unless you remain very strong about the level of impact and your involvement in the running of the business.

Just because you want to have a larger company doesn't mean you have to lose sight of your personal desires such as being able to work flexibly in order to have the family life you want.

Consider what you wrote down in Chapter One regarding what you wanted the future to look like for you and your business. We looked at the hours you wanted to work and the way in which you wanted to run the business. Is this still going to be the case when your business expands? If not, will you still be able to manage? Are you willing to change the way you work and can those around you support you with this? Alternatively you may find that, by the time you are ready to expand your business, your objectives or personal commitments have changed. For example, your children may be at school or have left home by then, giving you more time to focus on the business. If what you want from your business changes, by all means shift your expectations for it and act upon your new revised vision.

The key is ultimately to align your vision and ambition for your business with your lifestyle and personal ideals and goals.

You want to be able to enjoy your business, the flexibility that being your own boss should bring you and a lifestyle you have been planning for. If you enjoy owning and running your business, this rubs off on those around you, making your environment a more pleasant one in which to work and do business.

Wendy had been running her business part time for seven years when she had to make a decision about the direction her business was going in. She had spent too long dreaming about how she would one day run the business. Her life was too busy with work and other commitments and she hadn't given the business enough attention. Her business projects dried up and soon she had no real customer base. Wendy either had to give up her job and commit to the business to make it work or give up on the business and take on more hours at work.

Her need to earn a living meant Wendy took the job option and let the business go. If things had been different and Wendy had developed a marketing strategy and developed her customer base well, the business should have turned into a full time income earner for her. But it wasn't to be this time and Wendy finds her job fulfilling and less stressful to her than running the business.

LEAVING THE BUSINESS: YOUR EXIT PLAN
There may come a time when you no longer wish to run the business on a day to day basis. Just as you should start with the end in mind, you should have an idea early on how you will be able to move on from your business. Having it clear in your mind from the start will enable you to develop the business in a way that enables this.

When Joy established her salon she didn't consider the future and, when her husband retired from his job, Joy realised that the salon was a tie and she was therefore not able to take time off to spend with her husband as they had planned years before. Joy considered selling up and had the business on the market for 18 months, with no interest. She realised she needed to make alterations to the business so that she could take the time off she now longed for. Joy then had to recruit and train up a suitable manager and ensure the business could afford to pay both herself and the new manager. After much hard work Joy was able to take the well-deserved breaks she wanted and leave the business in the capable hands of a manager. Whilst this worked well for the business and Joy, it caused difficulties with her daughter who had hoped one day to manage the salon. Poor Joy hadn't factored that one in either.

With a good manager in place, Joy was able to demonstrate to potential buyers that her leaving the business would have minimal impact and she soon found a suitable buyer for her well run and managed salon.

Joy's story points to the various important factors when it comes to exiting a business. You need to:

- Decrease owner dependency to ensure that your business can effectively run without you.
- Consider potential successors early on. Put a succession plan in place a year or so before you intend to leave the business.
- Groom your company for sale long before you wish to sell it. Do this by considering who might buy the company and why, making sure you build the company to suit a potential acquirers needs and ensuring that it will stand up to a detailed due diligence process.
- Prepare well and prepare well ahead of showcasing the business for sale. Gather paperwork as early as possible.
- Sell at the right time – when you can demonstrate potential for additional growth after you have left the business. Try to attract buyers before you are desperate to sell – this puts you in a far stronger position.

As you develop your business consider how you can build your business so it can be run without you. Also consider what systems and processes it will need so that someone else could run it for you or buy it from you. Also think about how you will mange financially if you no longer run or own the business. Do you have any pension plans? Are you relying on selling the business to give you a lump sum for your retirement? Whatever you have decided it's worth asking an expert to help, to ensure you have the right plans for your future.

Keep in mind that this is your life and your business is your legacy. Whatever your plans for the future you have to do the here and now first, so don't get lost in dreams and forget about the reality of developing and growing your business. Being content and happy at any particular time in your business stage is important to ensure the continued success of any business. Keep reviewing your business against your business plan and personal plans and have an eye on the future, but don't take your eye off what is needed today. Aim for a balance between today and tomorrow.

We have followed Wendy, Lucy, Nicky and Joy throughout this book and they have each had very different journeys. Your journey will be different again. You are in charge of your own destiny and, if you set and believe in your own targets for success, you can achieve your dream and develop the business you want.

Keep thinking at all times:
- Is my business how I wanted it to be?
- How can I make my business be and become how I envisaged it at the beginning?
- What will make me happy and how will my business enable me to have the life I want?

REVIEW OF CHAPTER TWELVE

- Whilst you establish your business, keep an eye on the future and what it involves for you and your business.

- Have an exit and succession plan in place from the start that considers how you will leave, sell or close the business. Consider timing, management, resources, finances, successors and suitors.

- Think about how fast you will grow and what you'll need to do to realise your end vision. Make sure the correct systems and procedures are in place early on.

- Consider how you'll deal with the impact business growth will have on your work and personal life and on the business itself, including its resources.

- Groom and prepare your business for sale or succession long before you intend to sell it or pass it on to someone else to run.

- Don't forget why you started the business in the first place; it's easy to get swept up in the here and now. Revisit what you want and why.

- Align your business goals with your personal ones.

- Enjoy being a business owner and the benefits it brings you; you've worked hard for this, sit back and survey your success from time to time.

CONCLUSION

You should now have the tools I feel are important to you in business. I understand that you may have concerns about starting up on your own, worries about the financial implications or doubts about your ability. It's important for you now to reflect back on the journey we have taken together through this book. From it you should have learnt about you and your skills, your desire to run a successful business, the type of business you want and how you are going to get it. You now need to start on the next step of your journey, one on which you are never alone. Find other women who are starting up in business and share experiences with them, access support from your Local Enterprise Agency or visit my web site www.rebecca-jones.co.uk to see what you can do now to maximise your chances of success.

Good luck on your journey and please do drop me a line telling me how your business is going by visiting my website and clicking on the 'tell me about your business' box.

Remember, being a business owner can be tough but fulfilling, fun and so much more. If you develop your business in the way you wanted to, it is likely that you will develop as a person at the same time. It is not unusual for female business owners to speak about a feeling of empowerment and a development of self confidence as well as an increased personal control of their life.

Knowing you have started and developed a successful business, whatever that level of success, can help you overcome self-limiting beliefs. I regularly watch new business owners grow in ability and confidence. They now have more flexibility to earn a salary they feel suits them and their family needs. You can achieve your business dreams and give yourself the life you desire.

Good luck. Enjoy your journey!

Please keep in touch by visiting www.businessinredshoes.co.uk

GLOSSARY OF TERMS

Some words and terms you may come across while setting up in business.

Accounts - The formal documents showing your business financial affairs.

Annual Return - Summary of company structure, registered address and shareholding, filed each year by every company with Companies House.

Assets The items owned by the company such as shares, buildings, plant or equipment, vehicles and money in the bank.

Audit – An independent assessment of a company's accounts and records.

BACS -(Bankers Automated Clearing System An electronic method of sending money between banks.

Banker's Draft – A cheque issued by a bank itself, often used for making large purchases.

Bank Giro - A System of credit transfers, standing orders, and direct debiting.

Bankrupt - A person or company that is judged legally insolvent. A person can become bankrupt voluntarily or it can be forced by one of your creditors.

Benchmarking – A method of comparing a business against other businesses' performance in one or more specific areas. Often used as an effective way of identifying areas for business improvement.

Bond - A written promise to repay a debt within agreed timeframes and at agreed rates of interest

Breakeven - The point at which your businesses gross profit covers your overheads / costs.

Budget - This is an estimate of income and outgoings per month, quarter, year etc often set against an item of income / expenditure.

Business Angel – An individual who invests money into a business and who may be willing to provide hands on experience and involvement in that business.

Capital Gain -This is the profit made between the buying and selling of assets such as shares or property, Capital Gains Tax is the tax charged on such gains.

Capital Growth - The rise in the value of an initial investment, and any income that has been added to it.

Capital Investment -

Capital Stake - A share-holding or investment in a company.

Cash Flow - The cash in and out of a business

Commercial Mortgage -A long term loan secured on a business premises.

Contract Hire - A type of lease, often for a vehicle, where the leasing company takes a level of responsibility for managing and maintaining the vehicle.

Credit - Money received in to the business

Credit Control - Making sure that customers pay what they should when they should.

Creditor - Person or company who is owed money by your business.

Debit - A payment.

Due Diligence - detailed investigations often made by an investor before buying shares in a business.

Equity - The value of something, such as a property less any money still owing on it

E-Commerce- Business conducted over the Internet

Factoring – passing over your debts or debt collection to another company usually in exchange for an advance payment.

Grant - A sum of money that is given to your business without the need to repay the funds as long as you meet the terms of the grant. Often given during business start up or growth

Gross – Amount of money before deduction of tax.

Hire Purchase - A contract to hire goods for a specific cost for a specific period of time.

ICT – (Information and Communications Technology). Computers, Internet, telecommunications and other associated technology and communications.

Incubator - An organisation which helps start-up and small businesses to grow, often providing support and premises for an equity stake

Interest – The payment required for the use of money as a loan or overdraft; usually the interest rate is expressed as a percentage.

Investment - something you put money into with the aim of making more money.

Invoice Discounting - Selling your sales invoices to a finance house in exchange for cash. This is not debt management but providing a cash advance.

Liability - The money which people or other businesses owe to your business.

Limited Company – a company that is registered has shareholders and a memorandum of agreement.

Mutuality - Where an organisation is owned by its members without outside shareholders.

Net – Amount of money after the deduction of tax

VAT –Value added Tax is a tax charged on most goods and services by VAT registered businesses.

Lightning Source UK Ltd.
Milton Keynes UK
UKOW03f0804271013

219862UK00001B/15/P